smooth jazz

Arranged by Larry Moore

contents

ISBN: 978-0-634-02864-9

Visit Hal Leonard Online at
www.halleonard.com

Contact us:
Hal Leonard
7777 West Bluemound Road
Milwaukee, WI 53213
Email: info@halleonard.com

In Europe, contact:
Hal Leonard Europe Limited
42 Wigmore Street
Marylebone, London, W1U 2RN
Email: info@halleonardeurope.com

In Australia, contact:
Hal Leonard Australia Pty. Ltd.
4 Lentara Court
Cheltenham, Victoria, 3192 Australia
Email: info@halleonard.com.au

ANGELA
Theme from the Paramount Television Series TAXI

By BOB JAMES

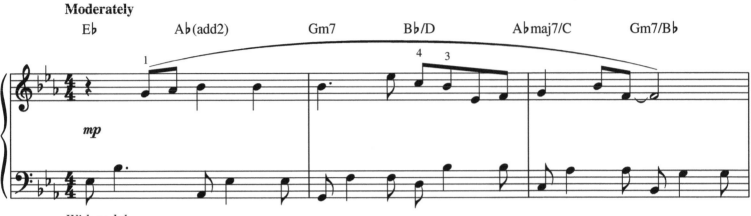

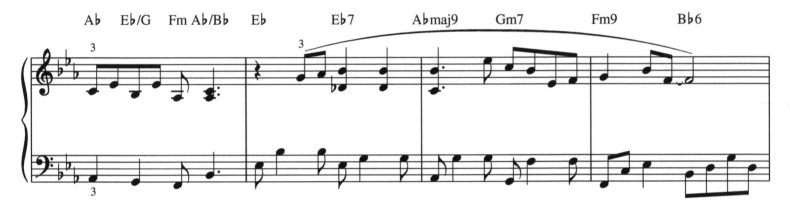

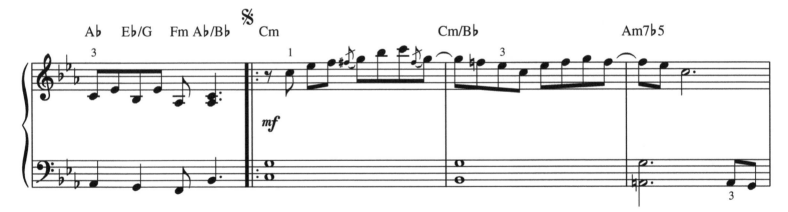

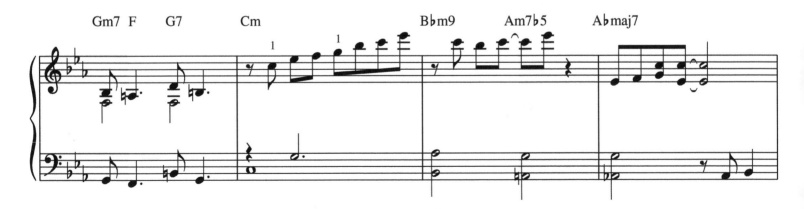

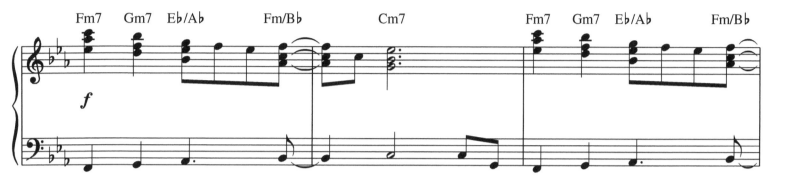

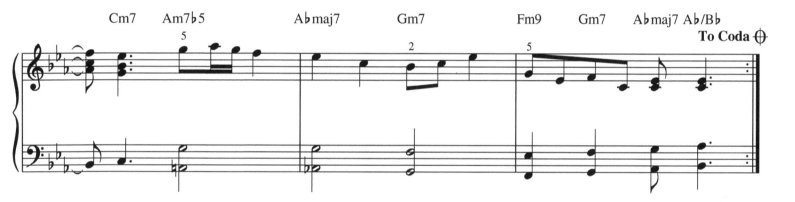

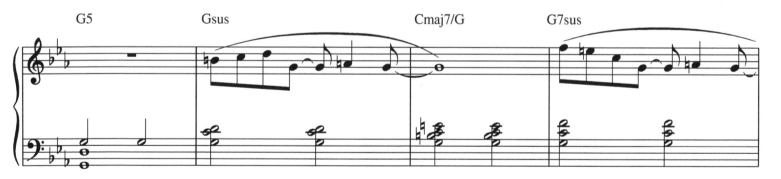

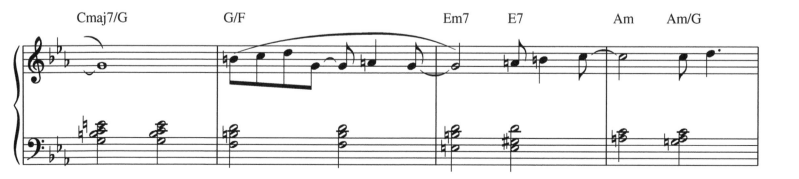

4

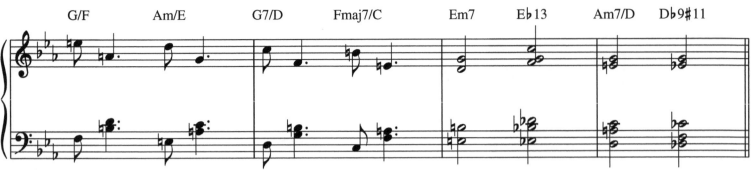

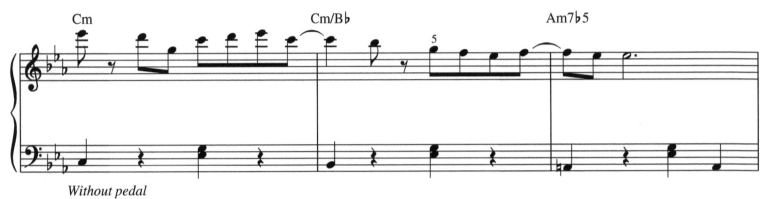

Cm   Cm/B♭   Am7♭5

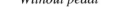
Without pedal

A♭maj7   Cm   B♭7   Am7♭5   A♭maj7

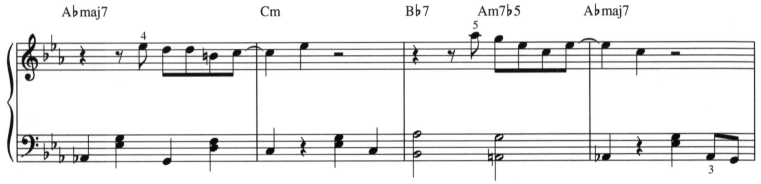

F7sus   Gm7   Cm   Cm/B♭   Am7♭5

A♭maj7   Gm7   Cm7   B♭7   F(add2)/A   A♭maj7

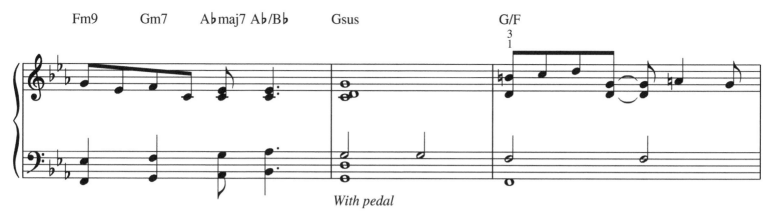

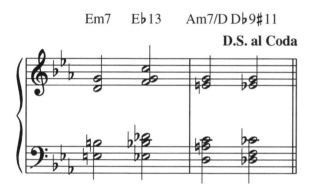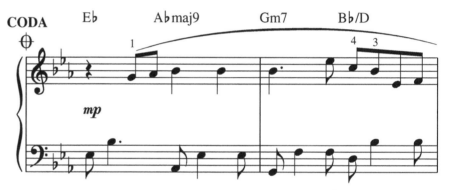

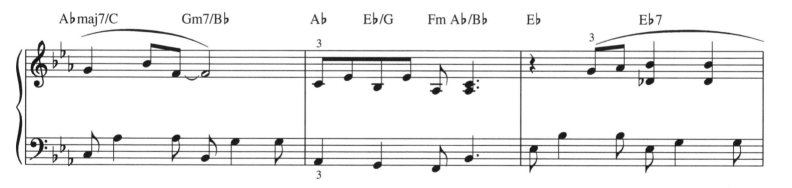

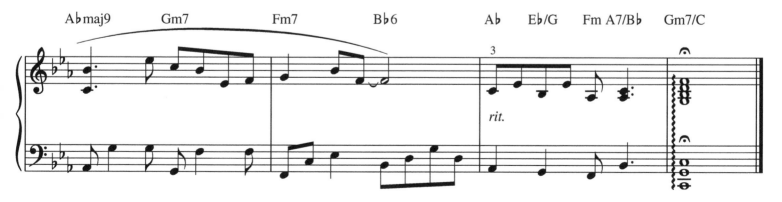

BABY, COME TO ME

Words and Music by
ROD TEMPERTON

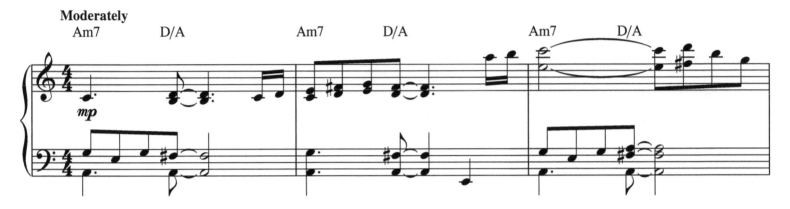

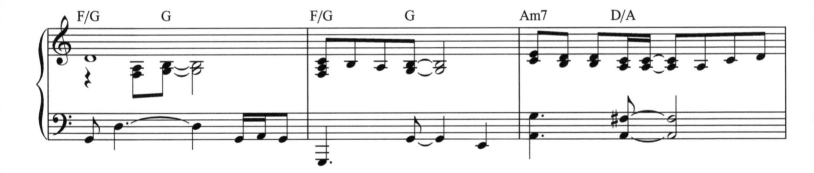

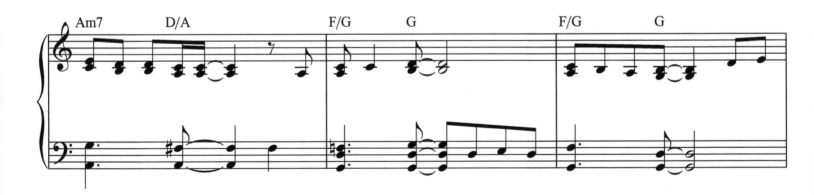

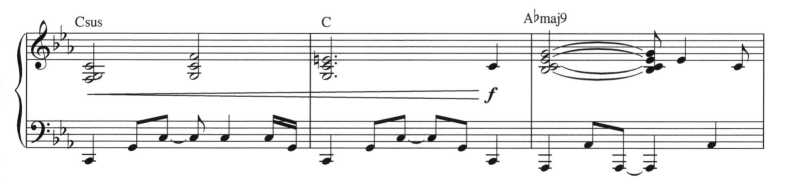

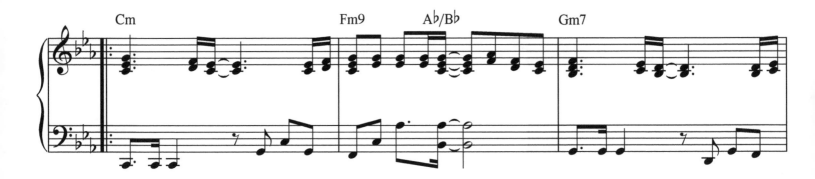

BALI RUN

By LEE RITENOUR
and BOB JAMES

Moderately fast

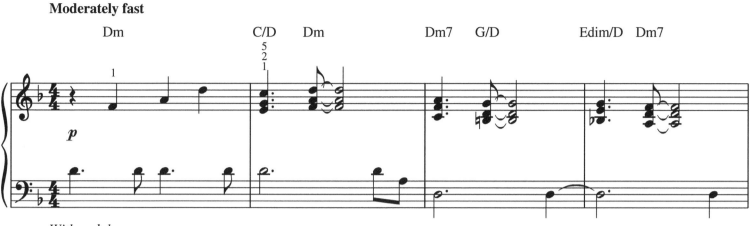

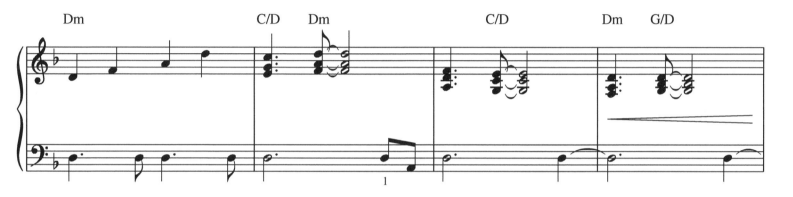

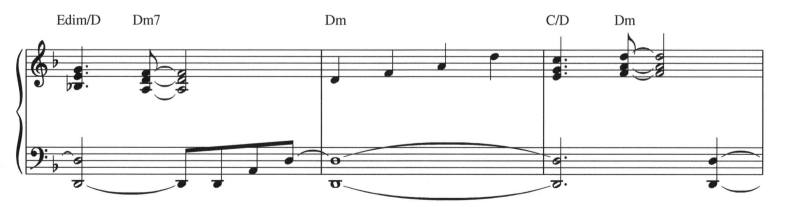

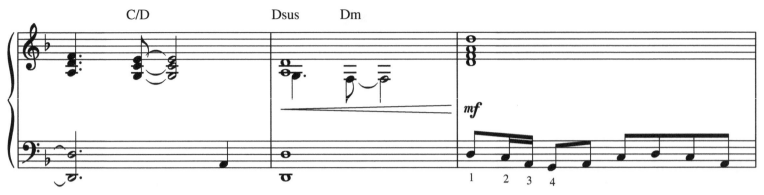

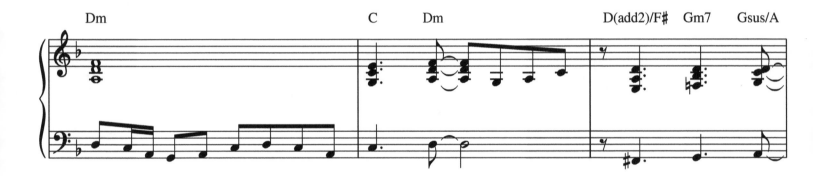

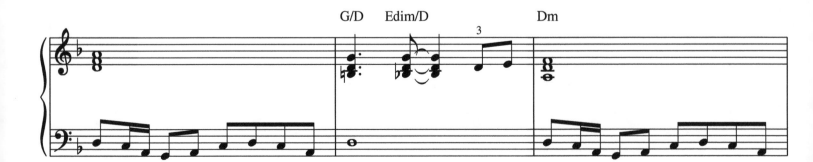

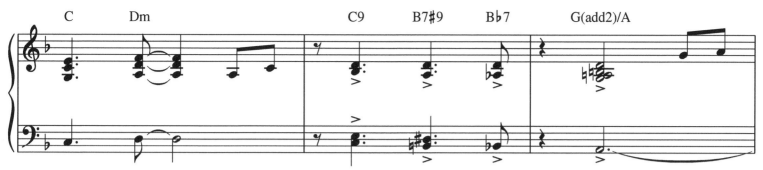

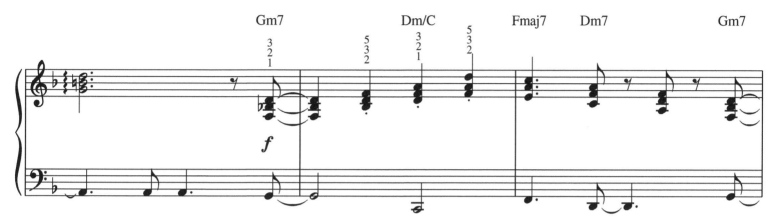

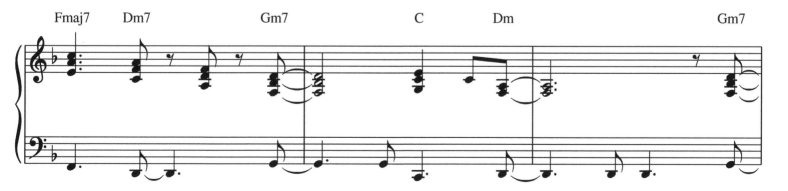

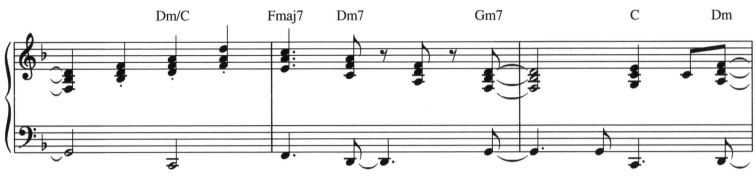

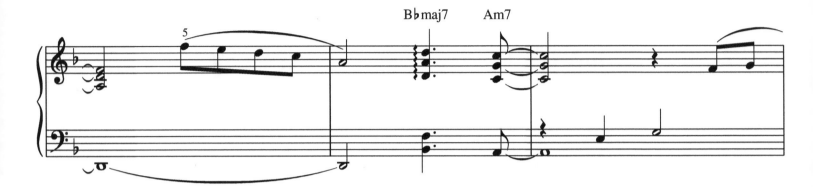

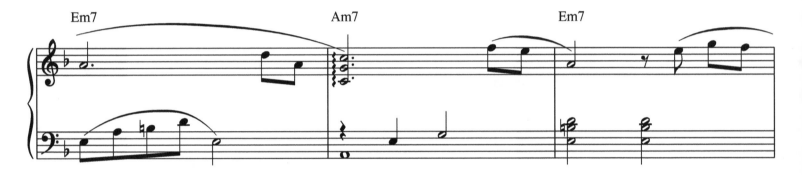

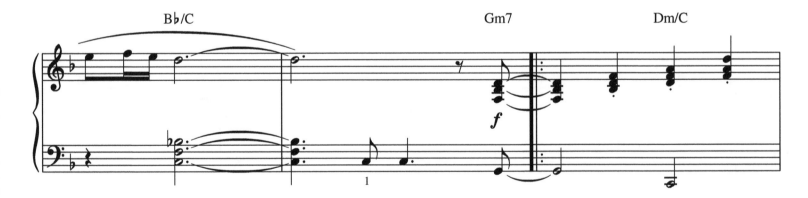

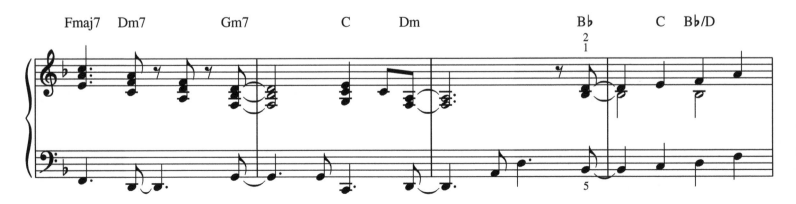

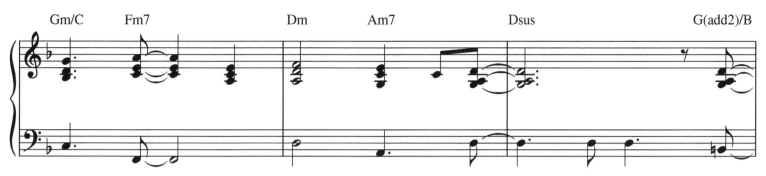

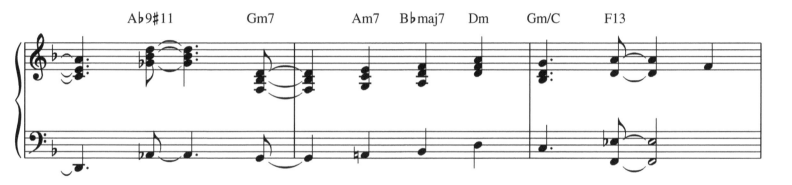

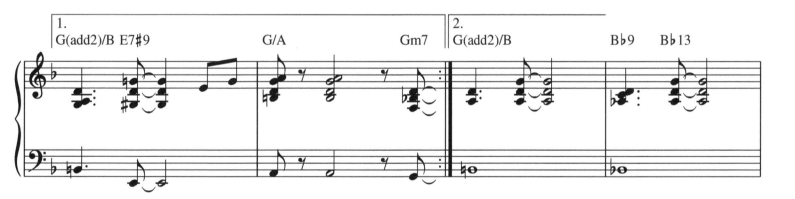

CAST YOUR FATE TO THE WIND

Music by VINCE GUARALDI

Moderately, with a beat

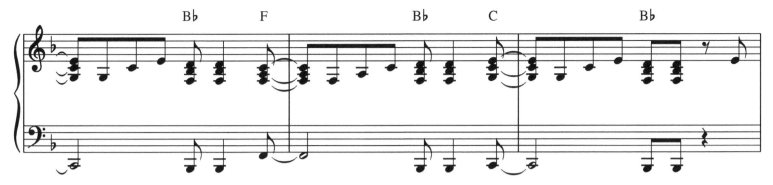

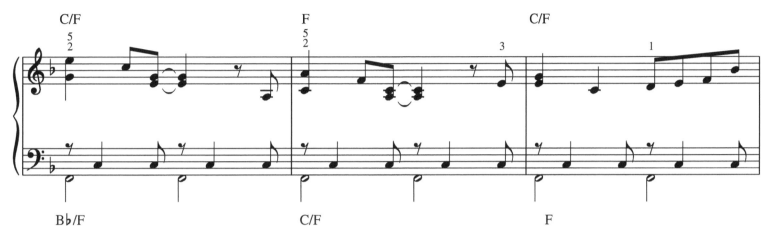

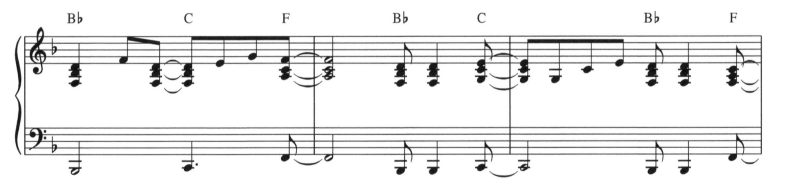

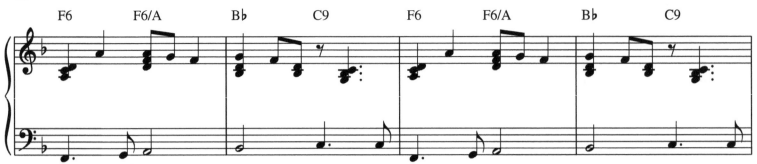

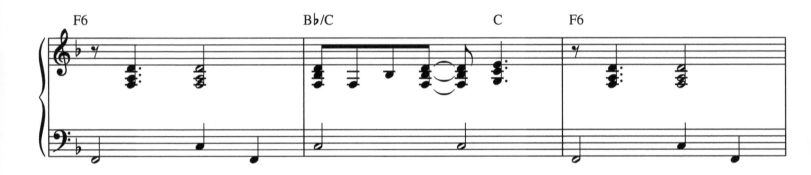

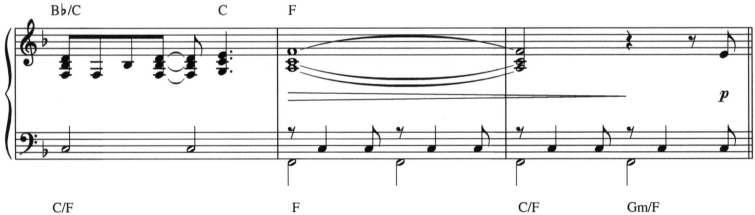

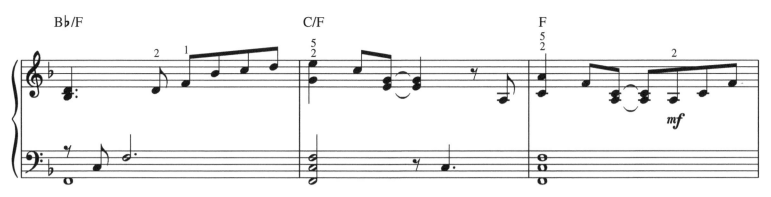

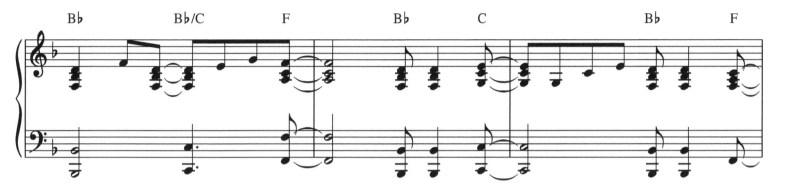

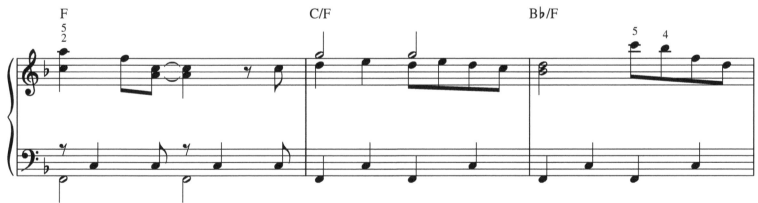

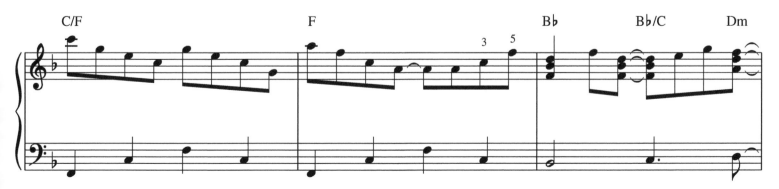

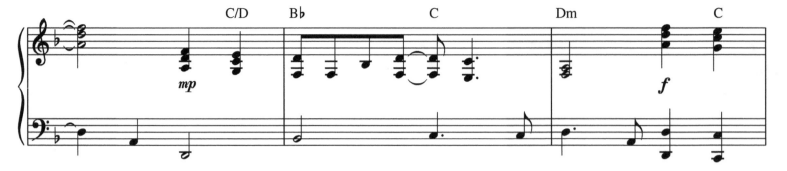

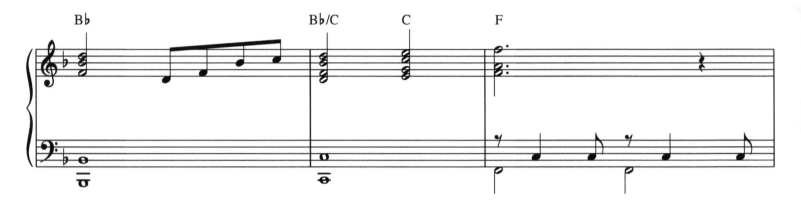

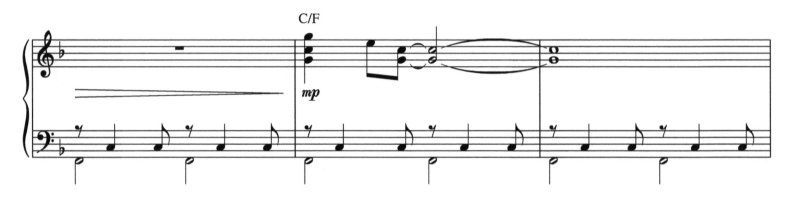

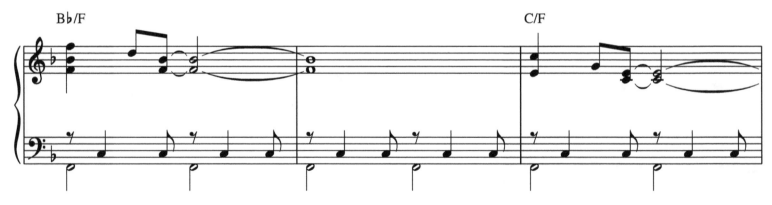

JUST THE TWO OF US

Words and Music by RALPH MacDONALD,
WILLIAM SALTER and BILL WITHERS

Moderately

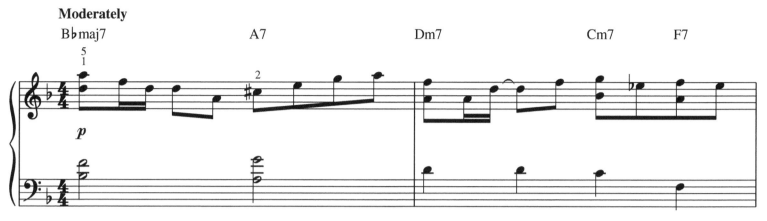

With pedal

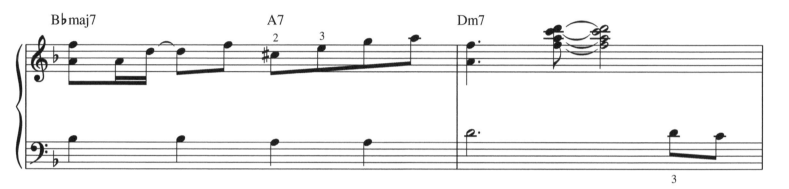

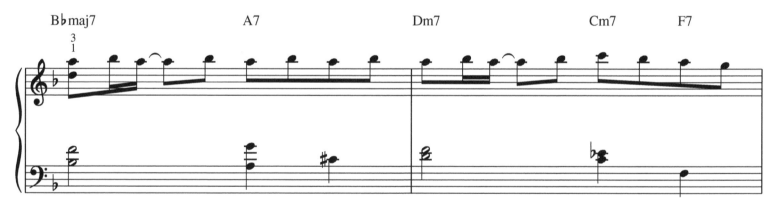

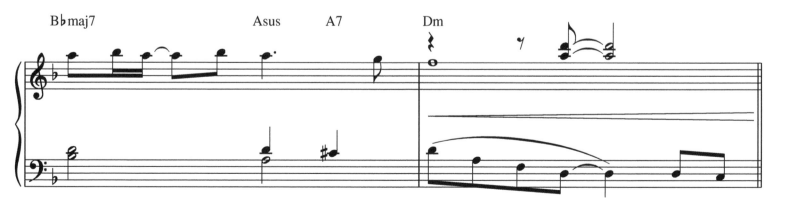

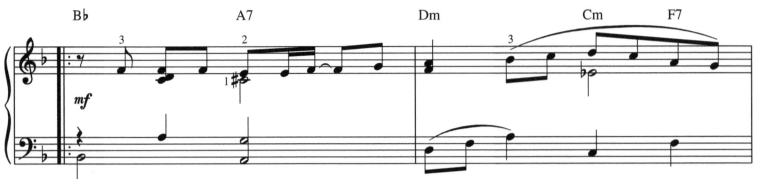

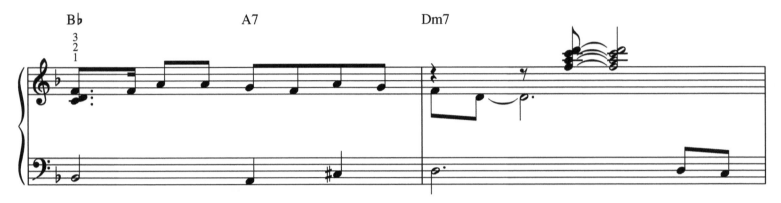

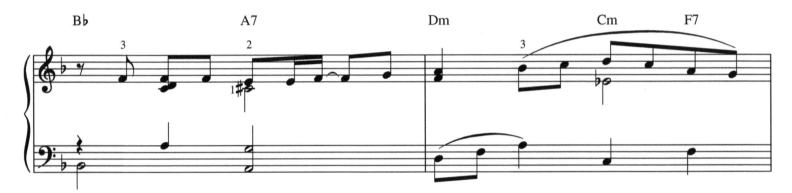

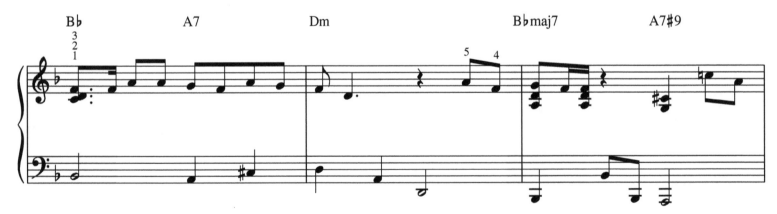

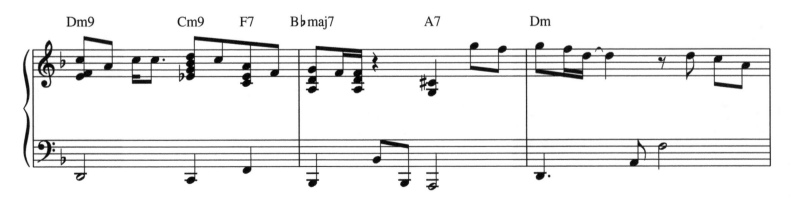

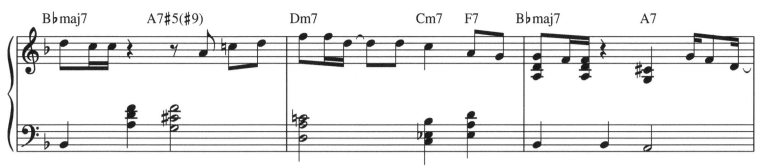

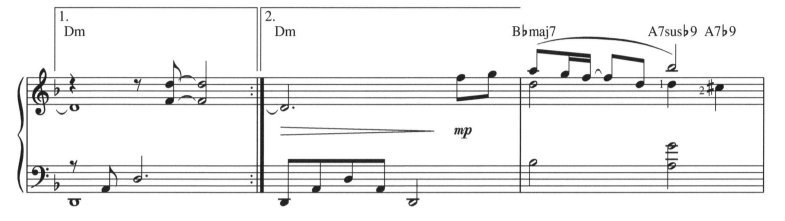

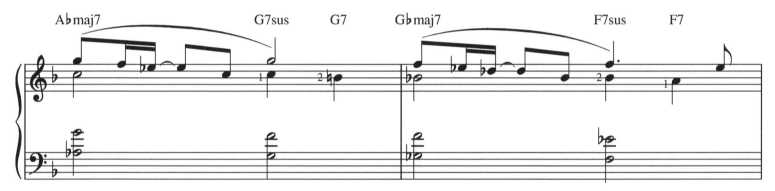

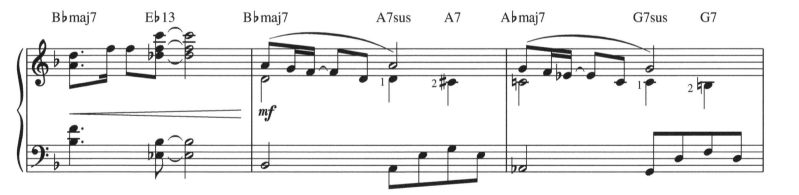

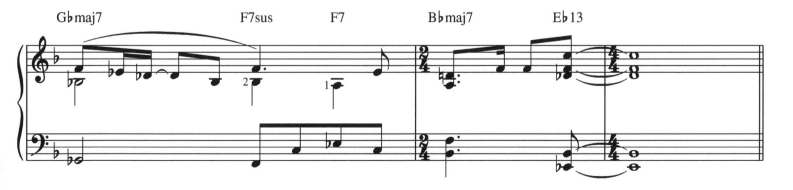

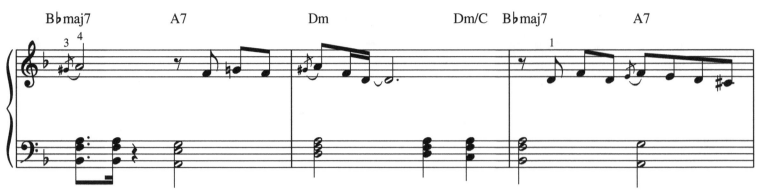

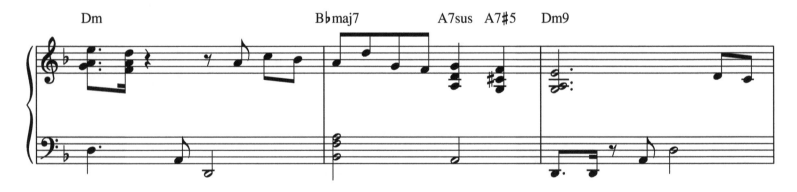

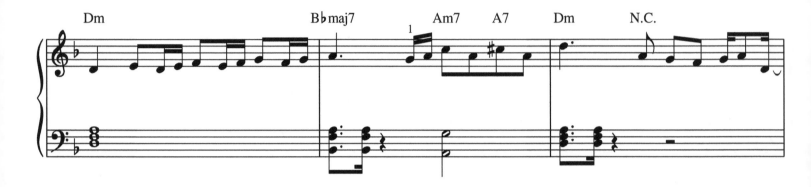

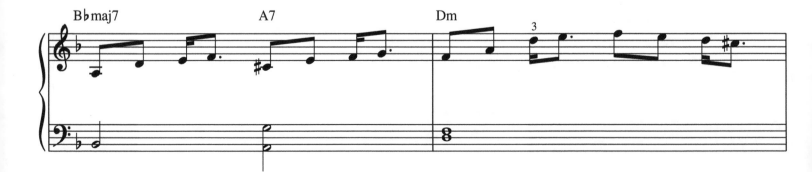

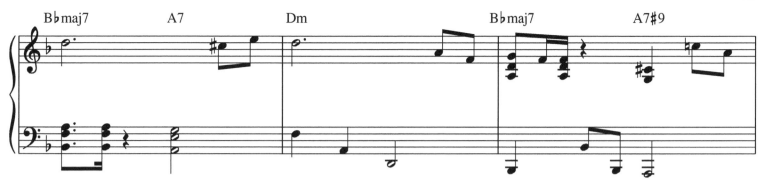

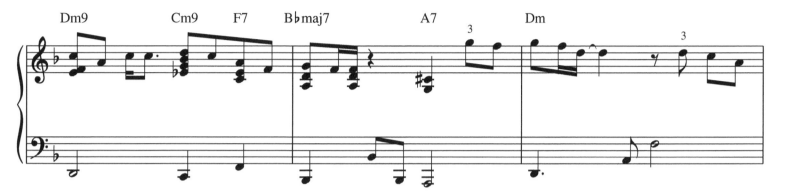

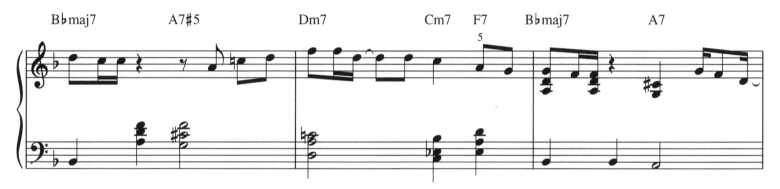

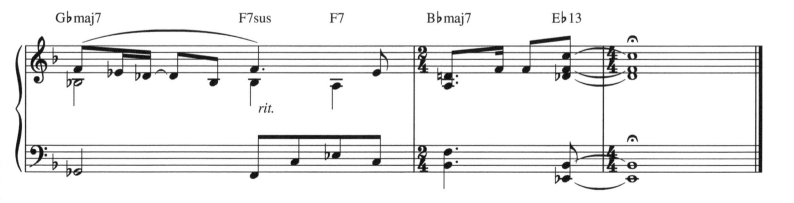

HARLEM NOCTURNE

Music by EARLE HAGEN

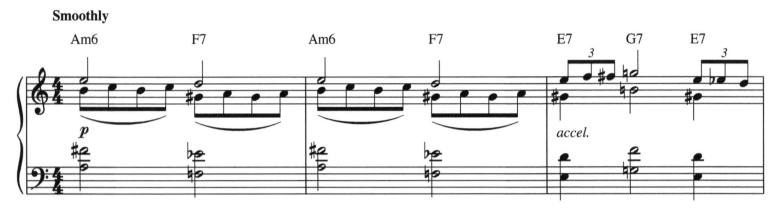

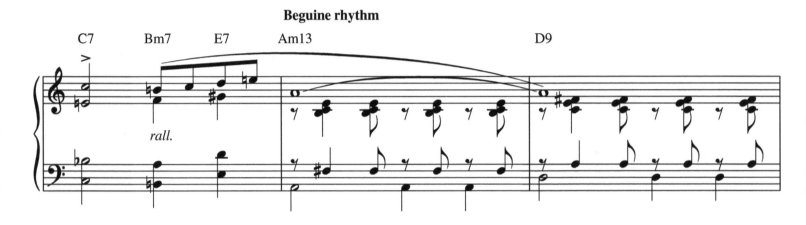

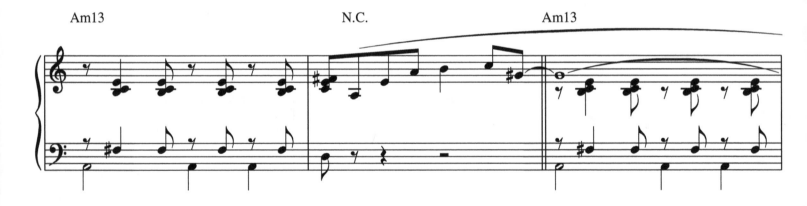

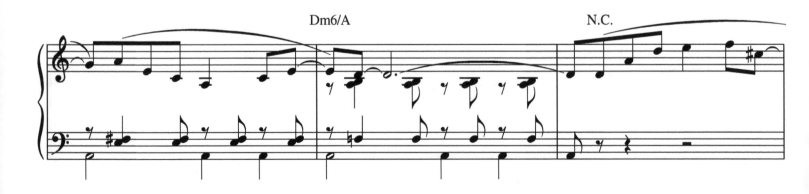

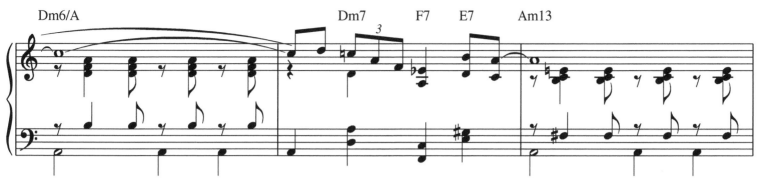

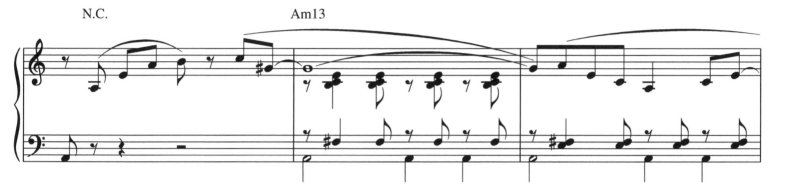

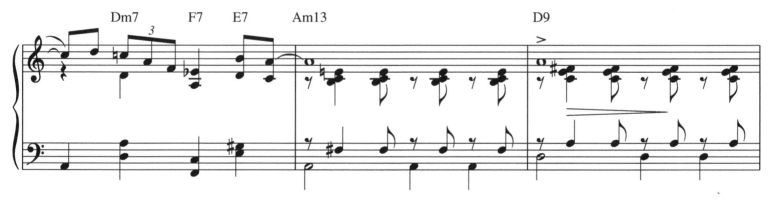

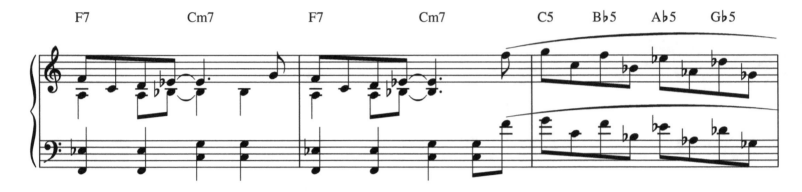

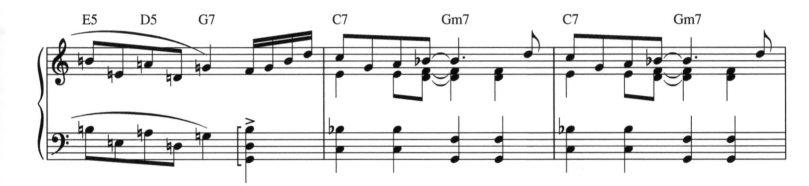

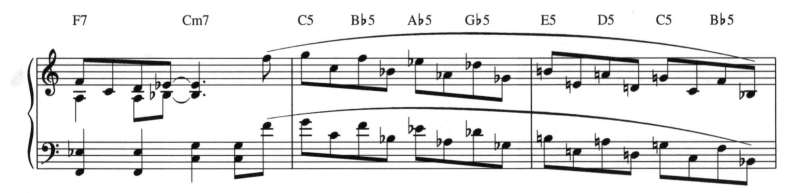

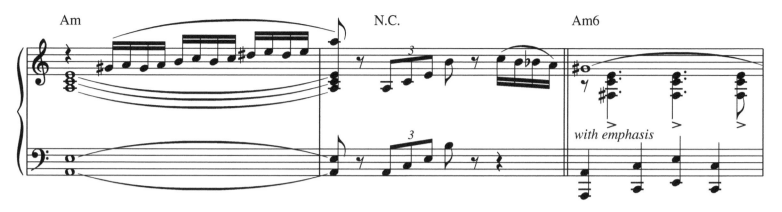

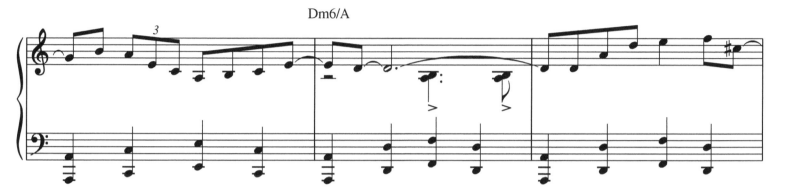

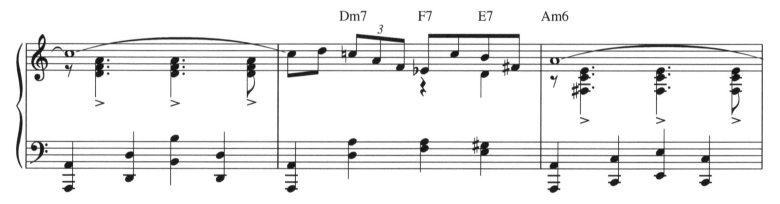

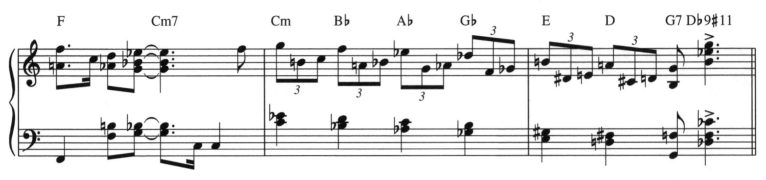

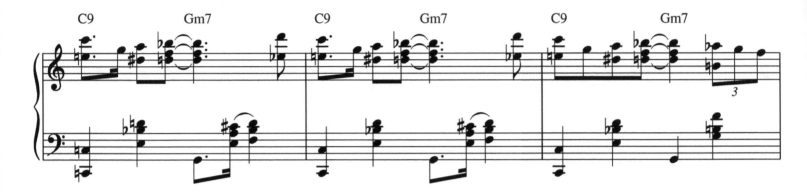

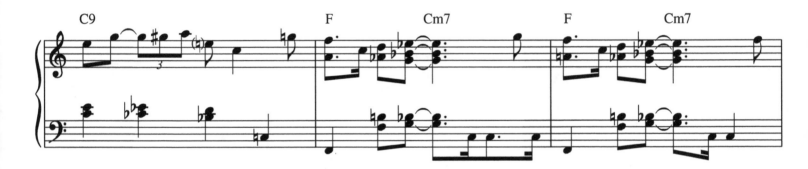

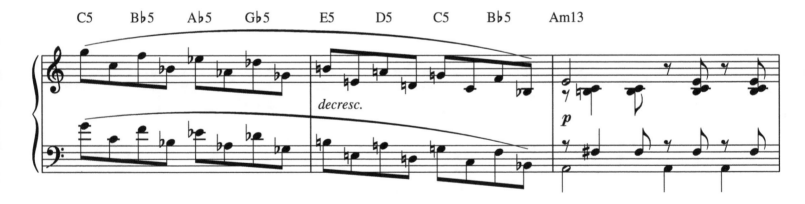

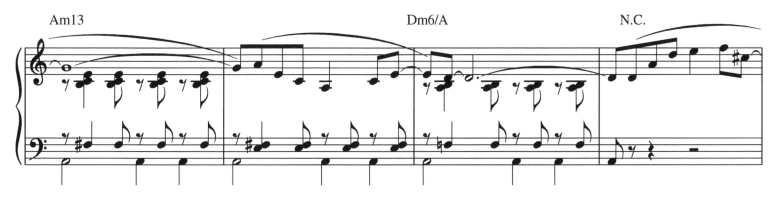

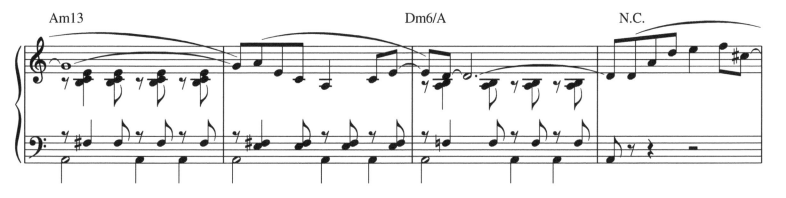

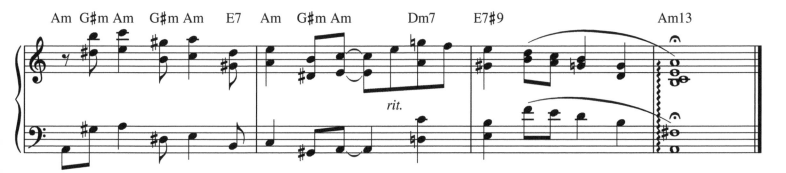

HOME

By KENNY G

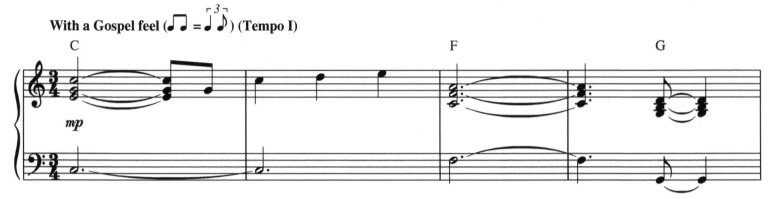

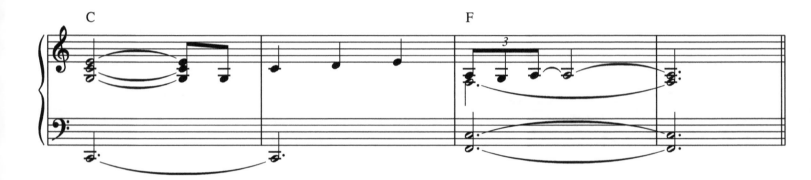

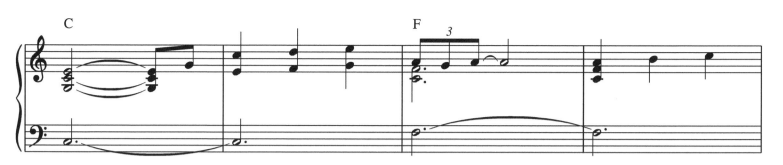

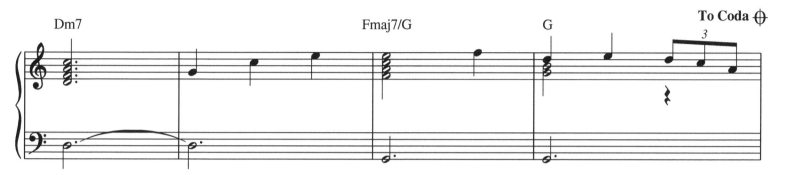

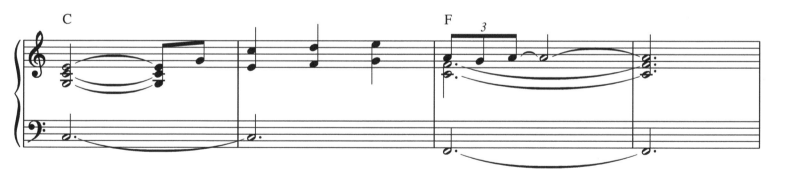

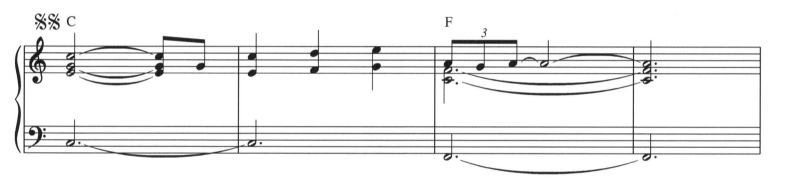

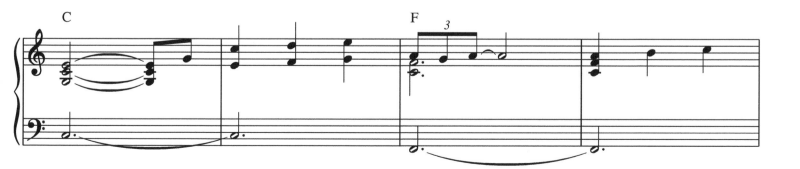

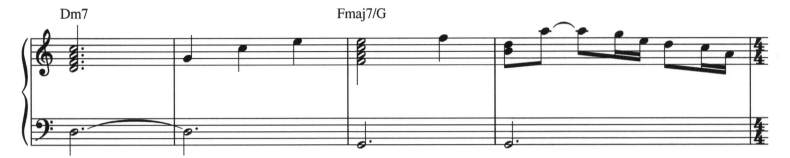

Moderately (not too fast) (Tempo II)

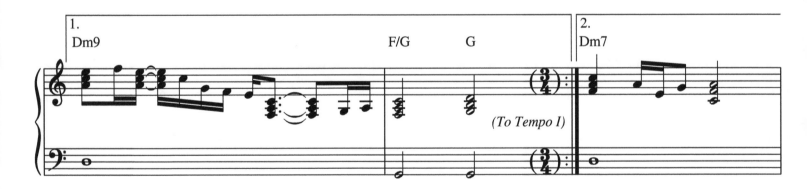

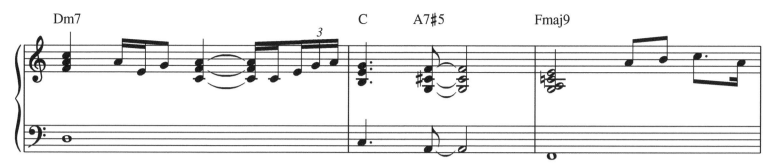

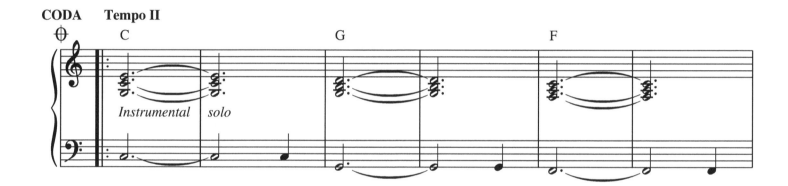

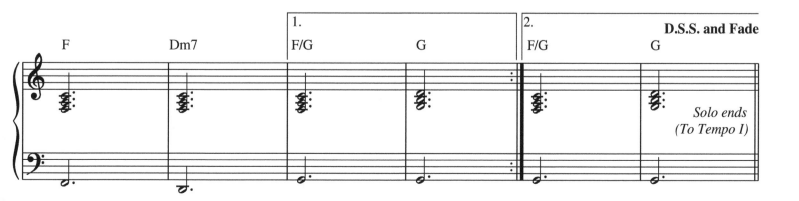

MINUTE BY MINUTE

Words and Music by MICHAEL McDONALD
and LESTER ABRAMS

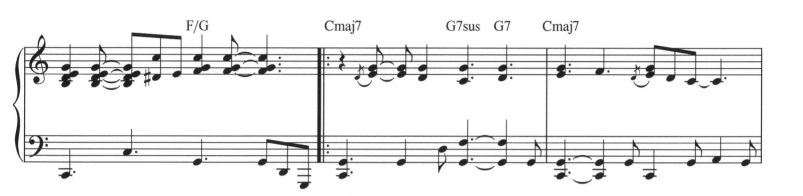

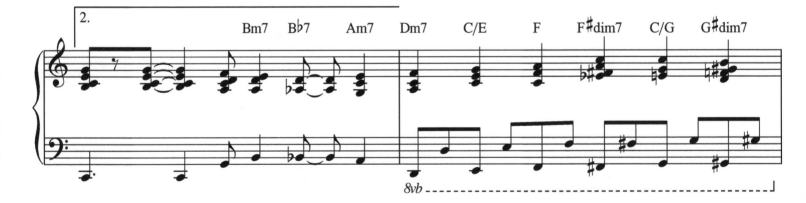

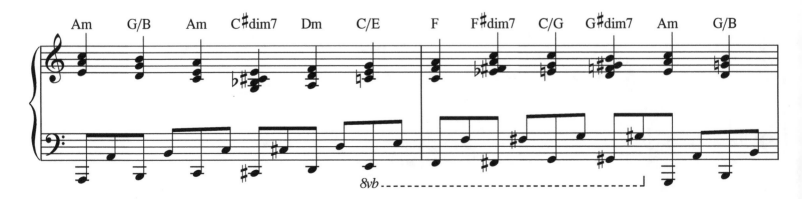

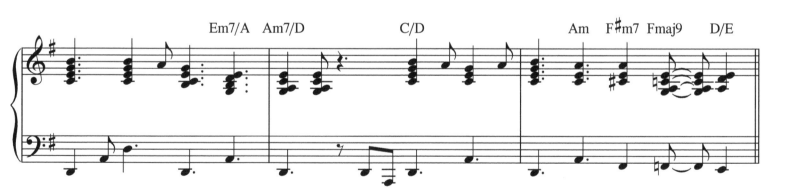

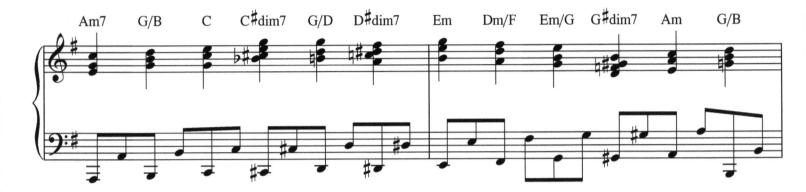

MOUNTAIN DANCE

By DAVE GRUSIN

Moderately fast

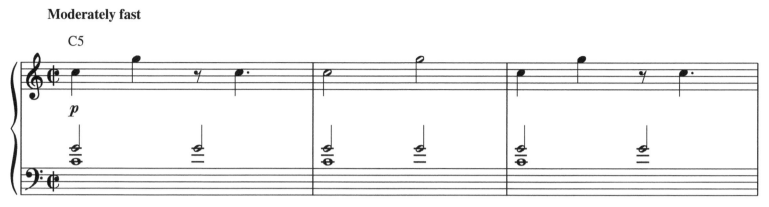

With pedal

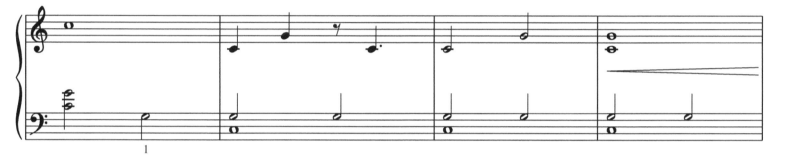

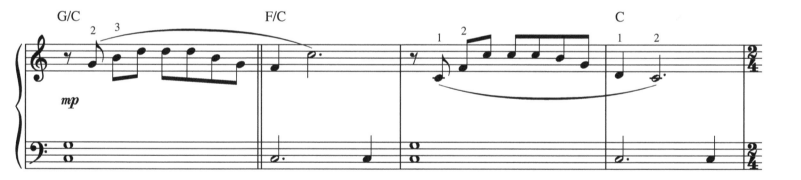

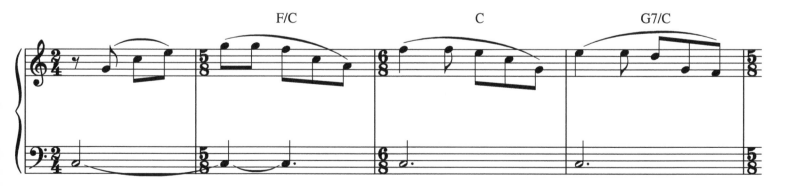

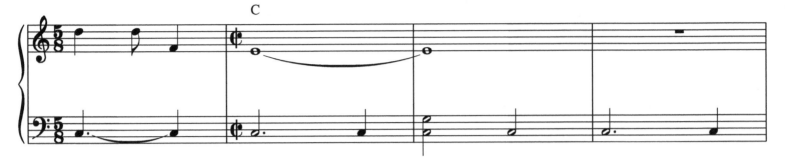

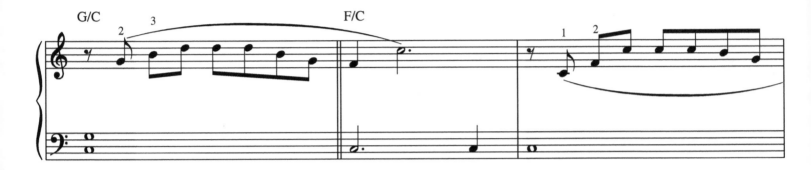

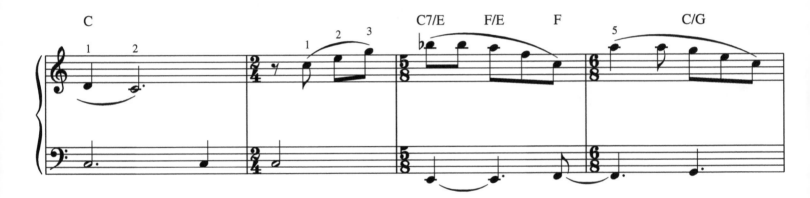

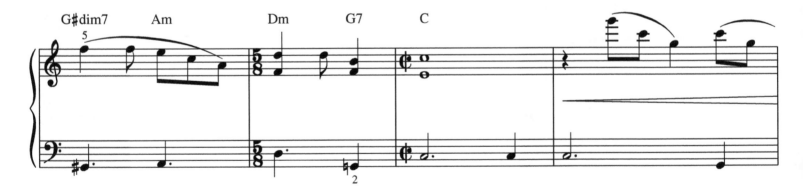

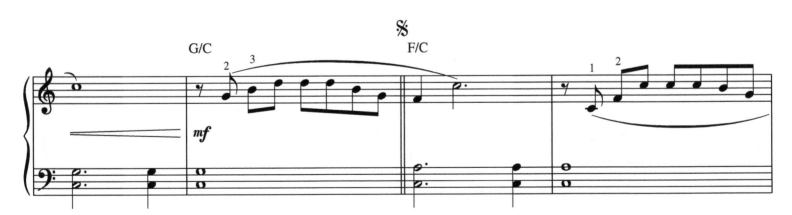

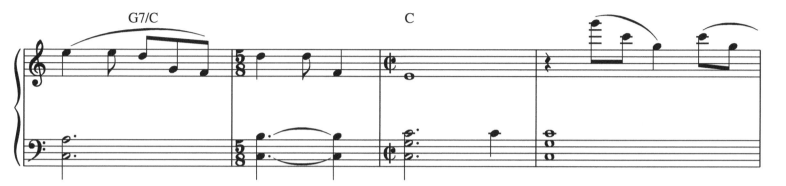

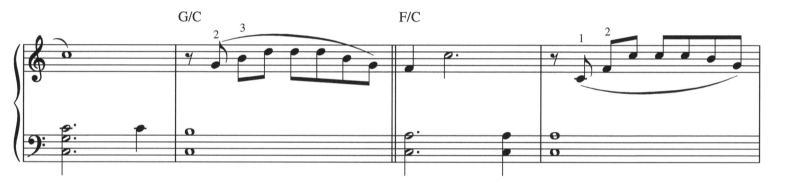

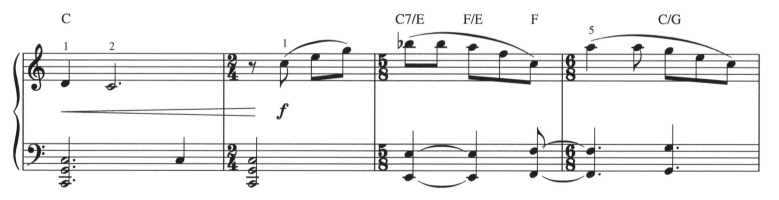

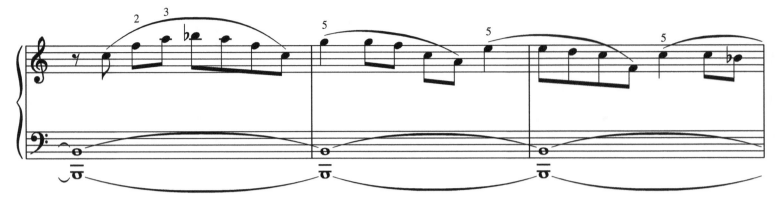

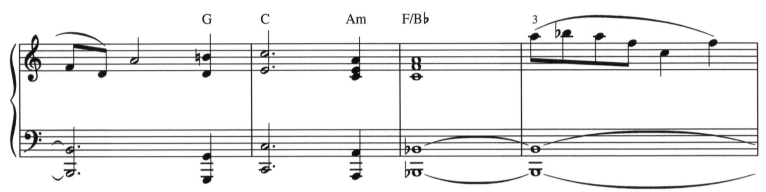

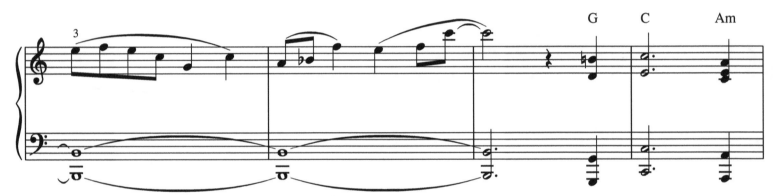

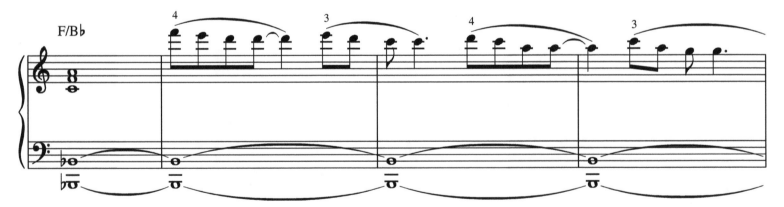

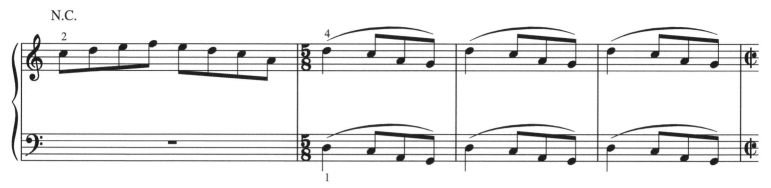

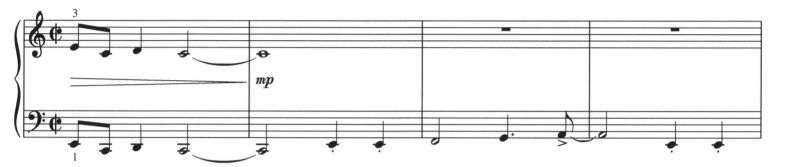

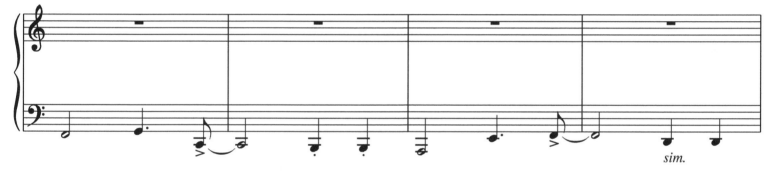

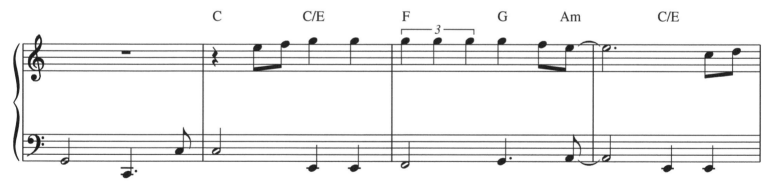

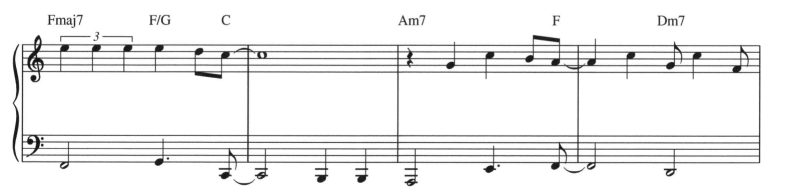

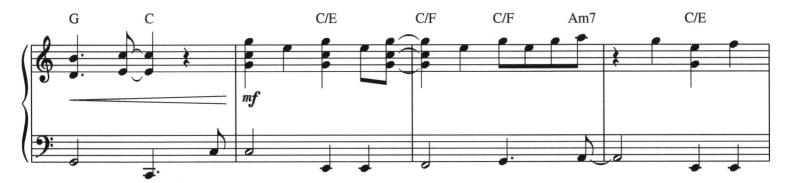

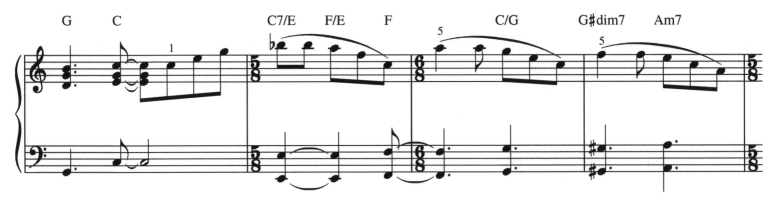

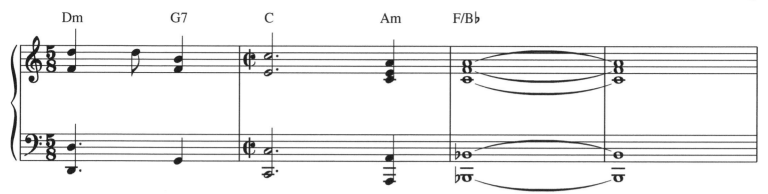

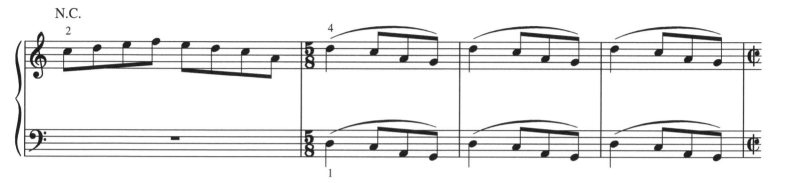

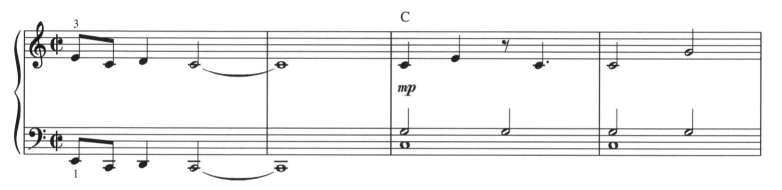

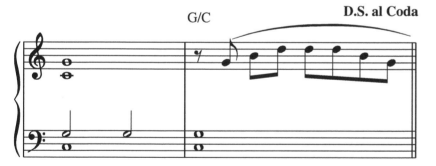

MR. MAGIC

Words and Music by RALPH MacDONALD
and WILLIAM SALTER

Moderate Funk

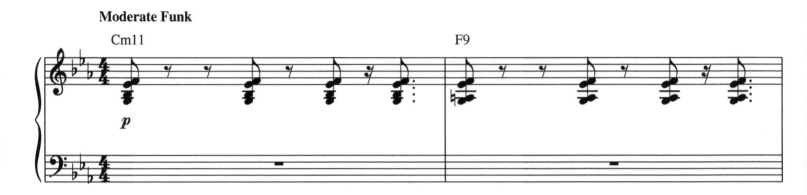

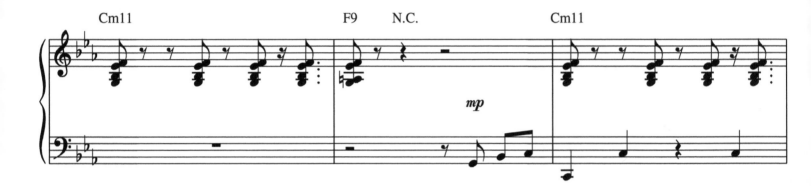

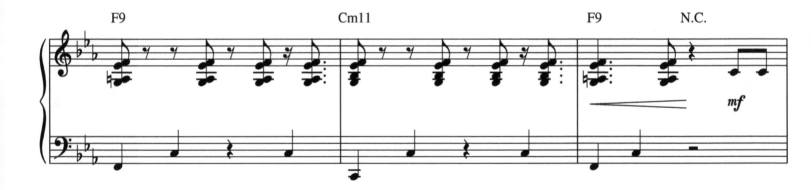

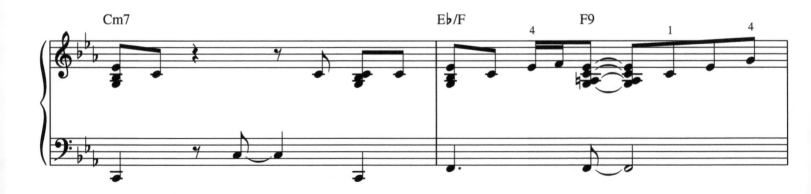

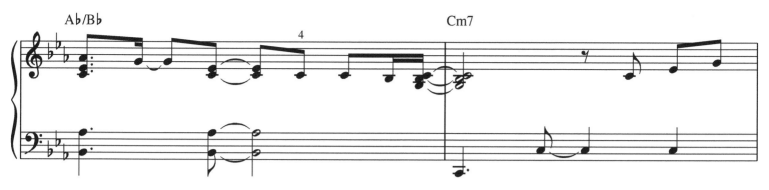

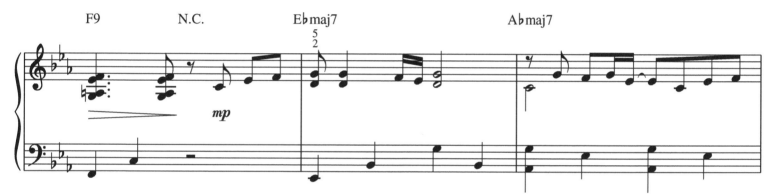

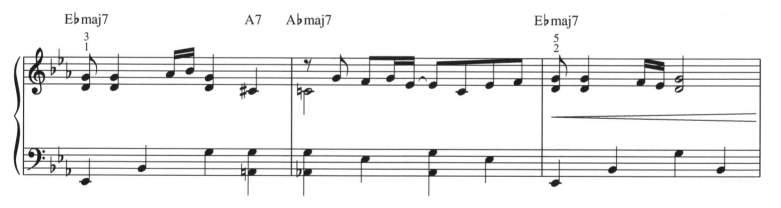

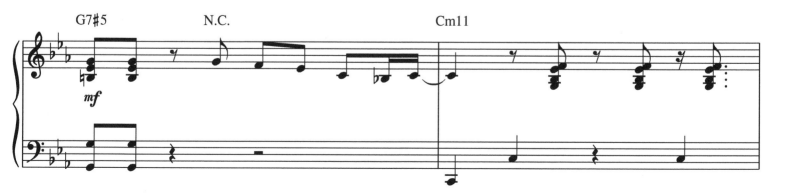

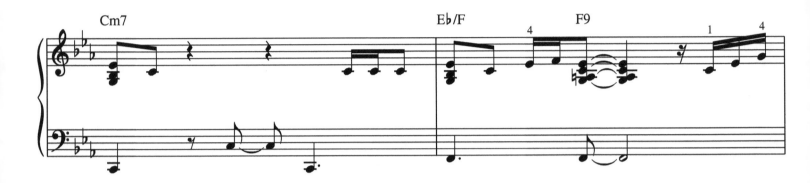

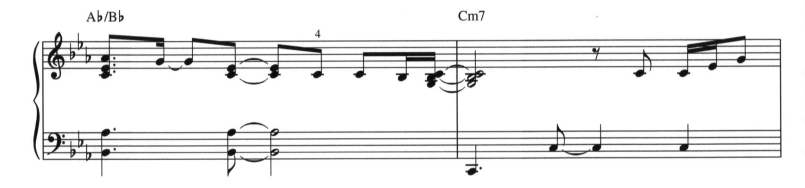

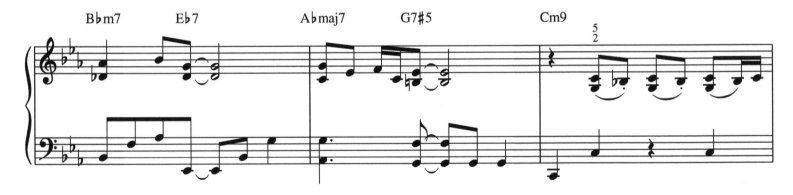

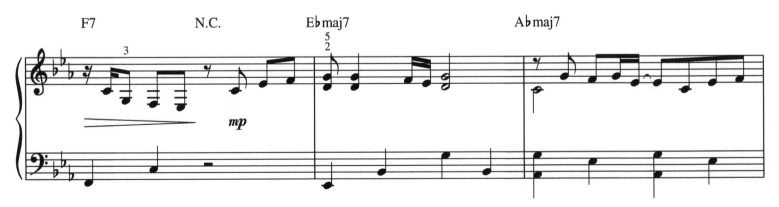

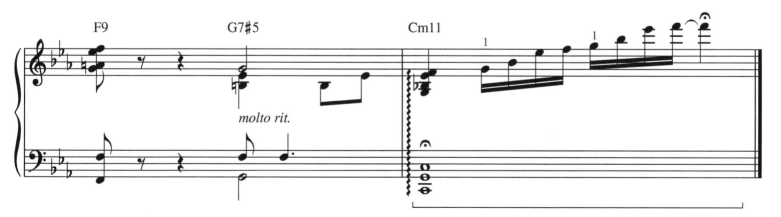

MORNING DANCE

By JAY BECKENSTEIN

Moderate Latin

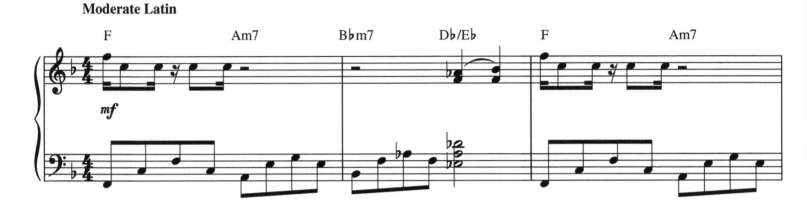

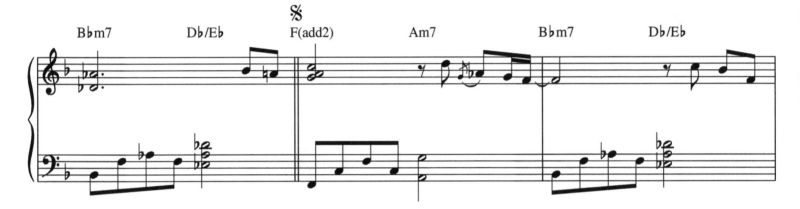

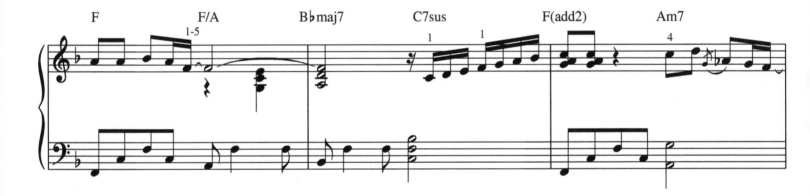

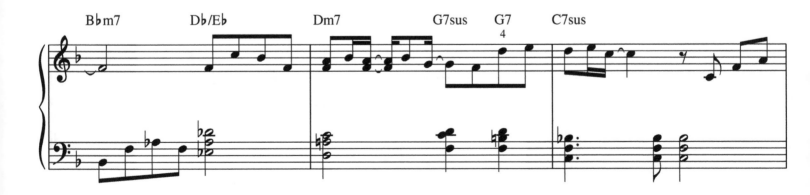

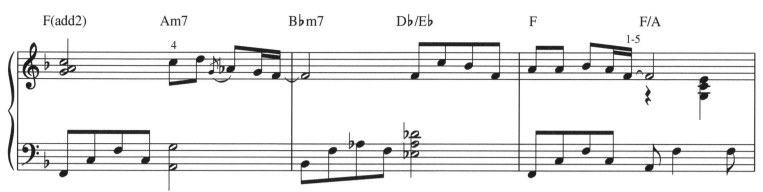

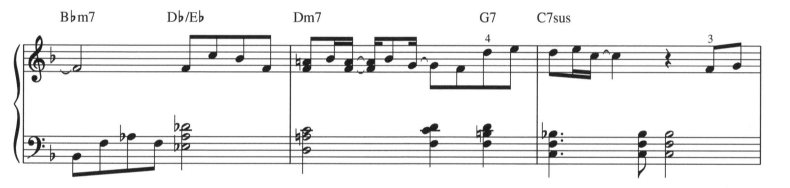

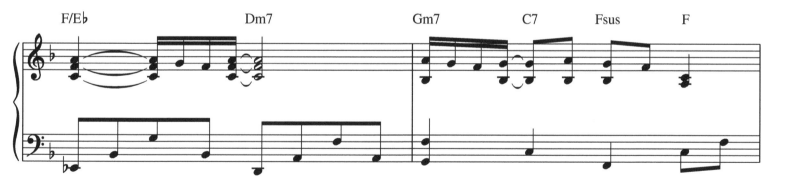

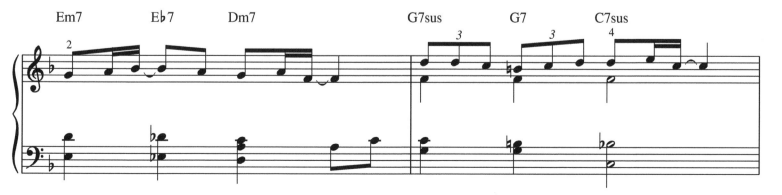

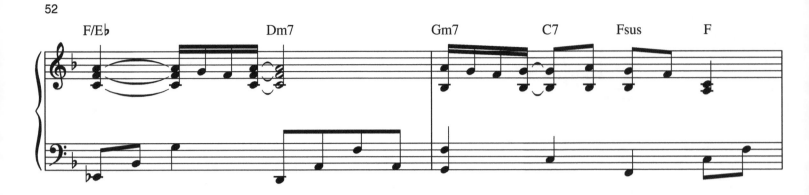

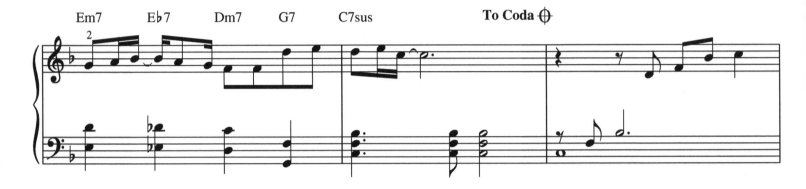

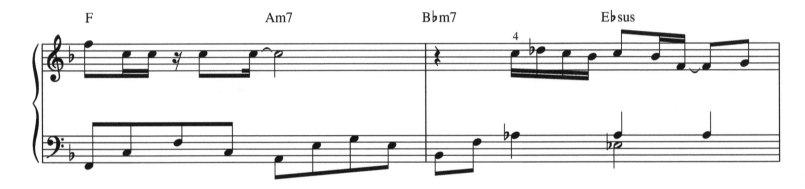

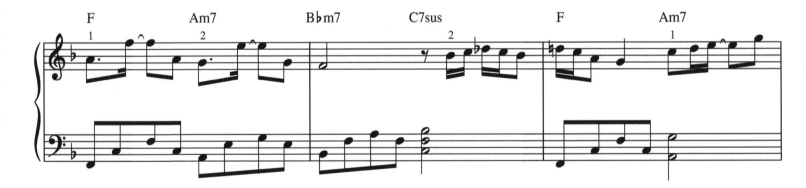

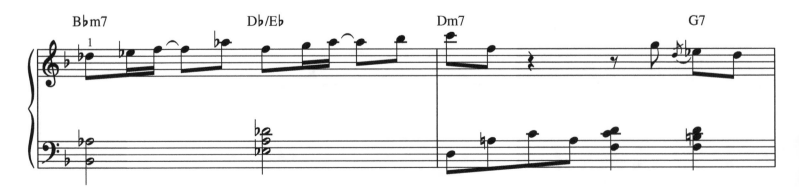

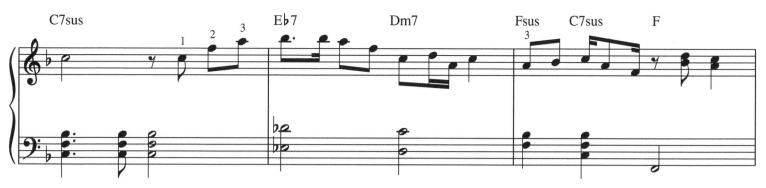

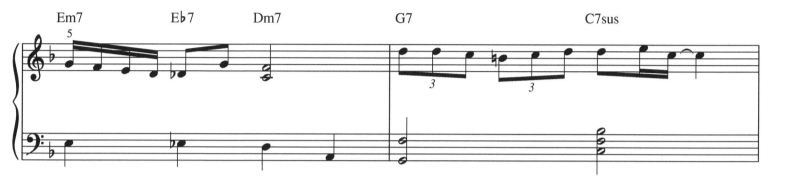

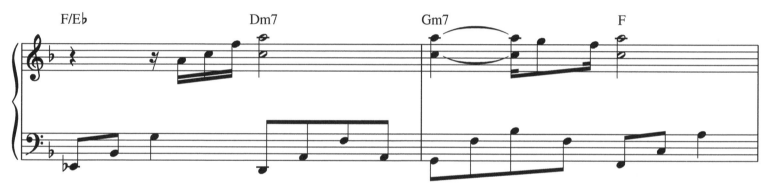

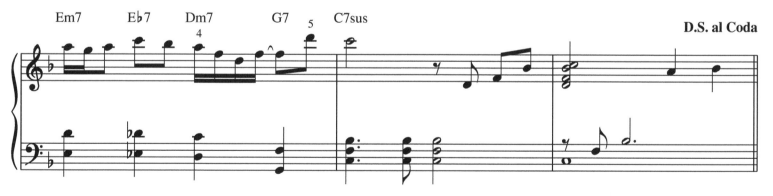

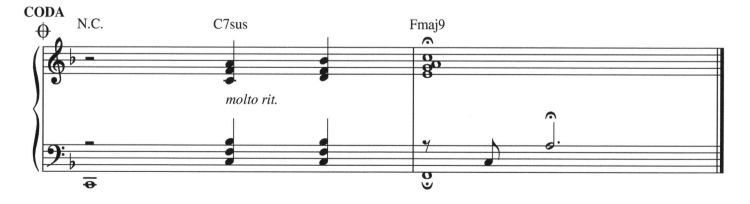

RIO DE JANEIRO BLUE

Words and Music by RICHARD TORRANCE
and JOHN HAENY

Moderately fast Latin

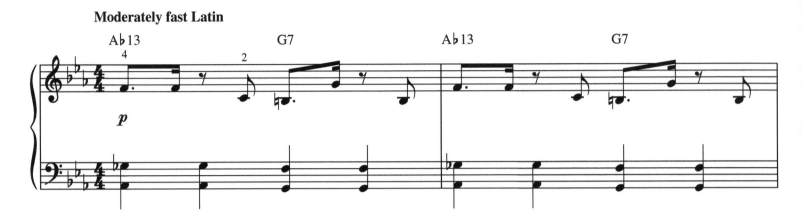

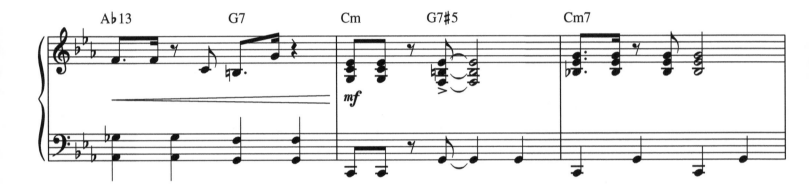

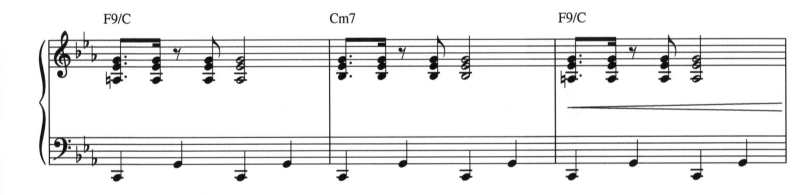

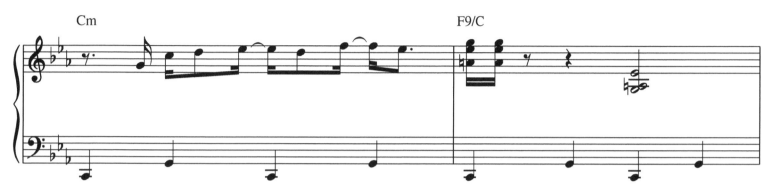

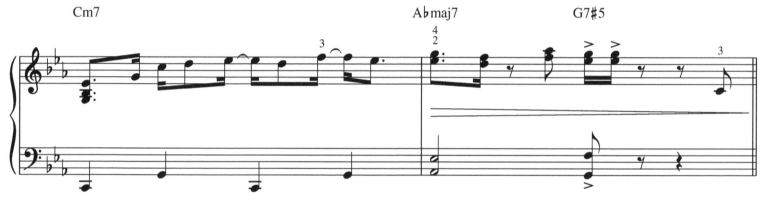

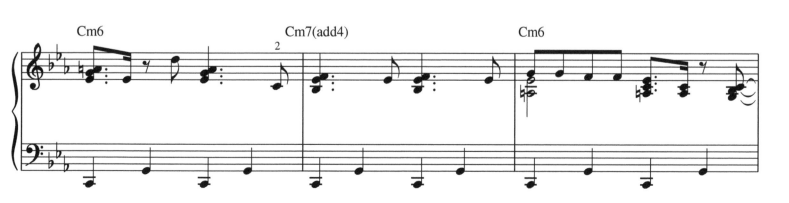

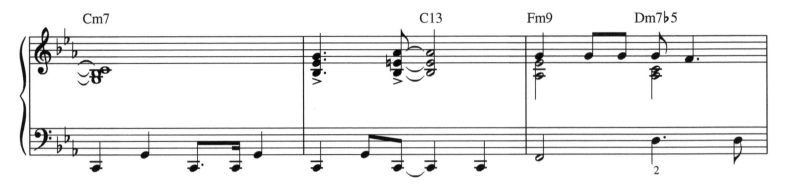

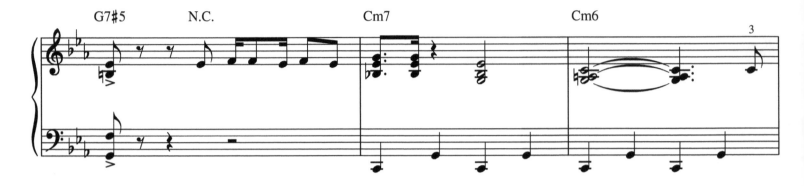

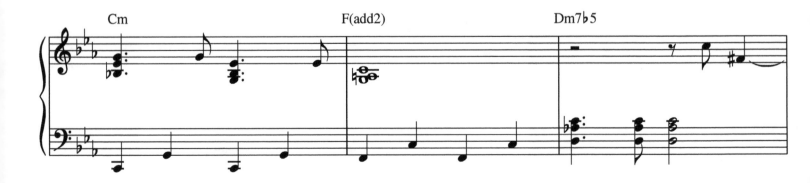

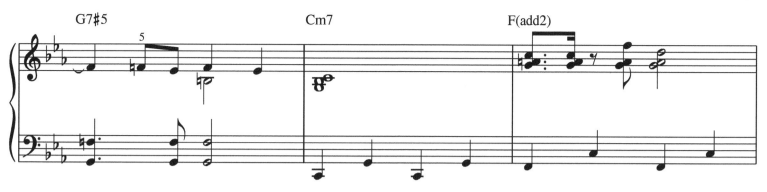

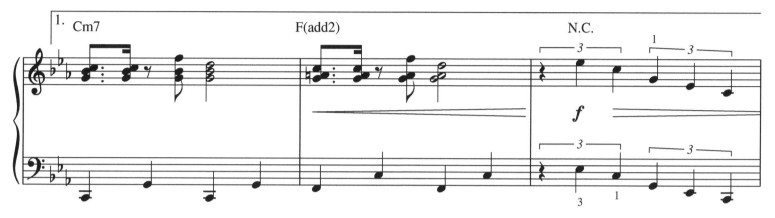

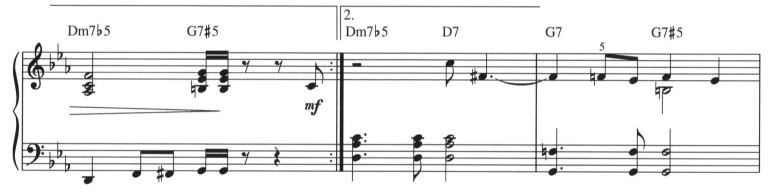

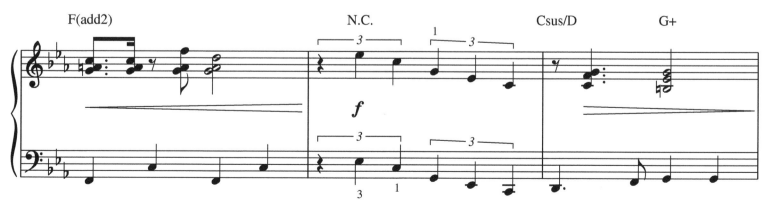

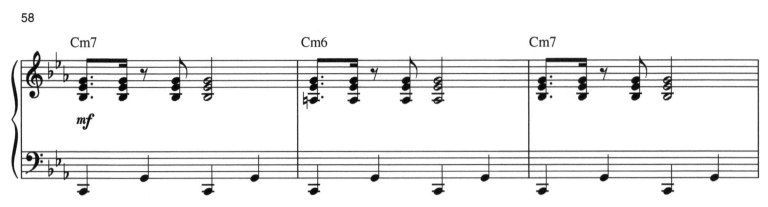

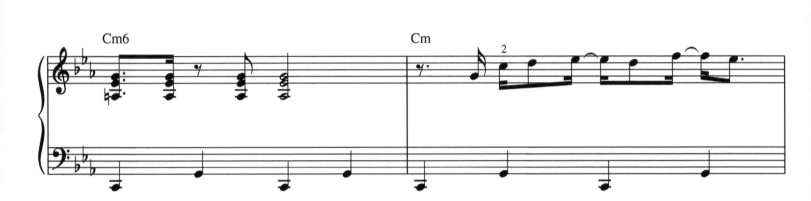

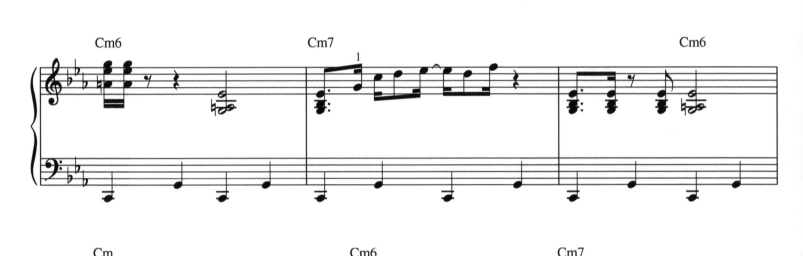

SHE LIKES TO WATCH

By RUSS FREEMAN

Moderate Funk Rock

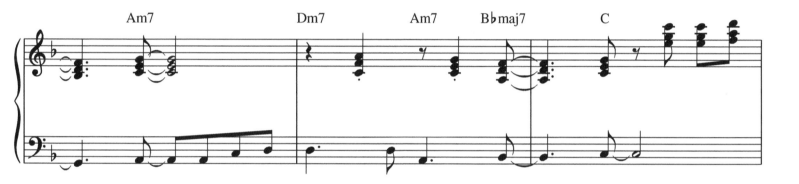

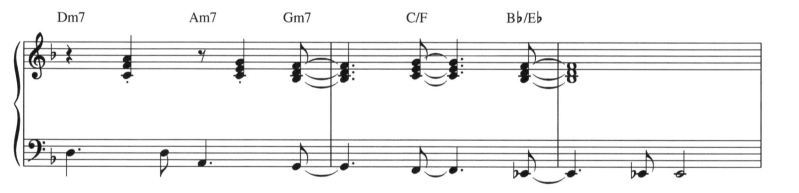

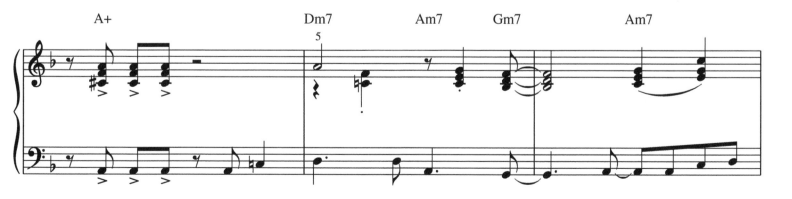

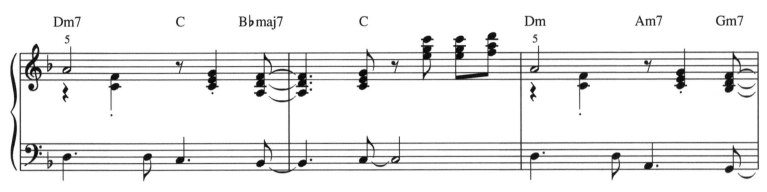

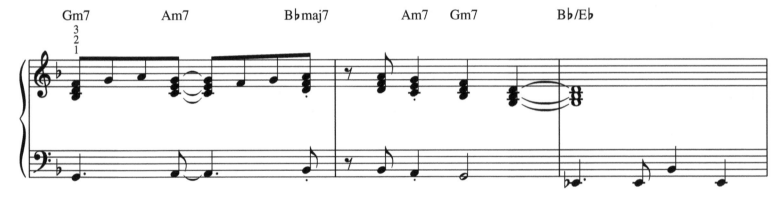

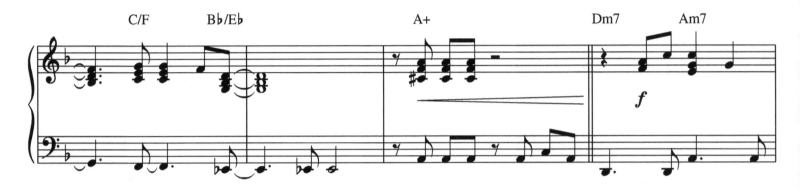

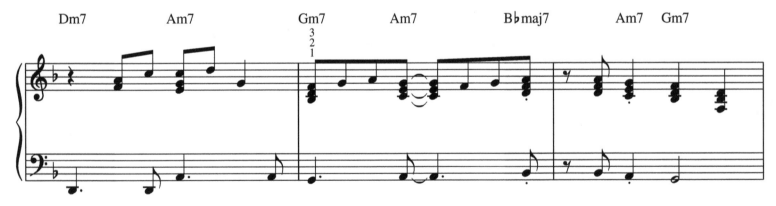

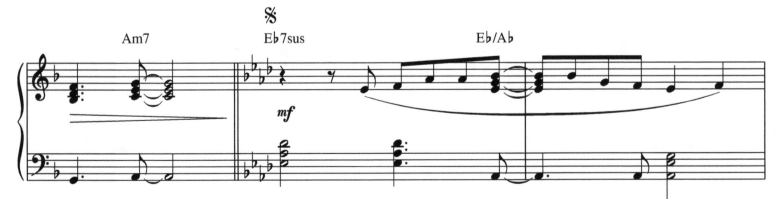

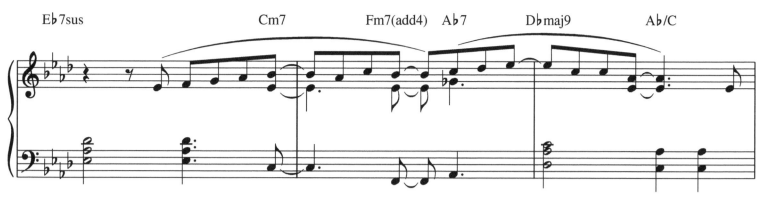

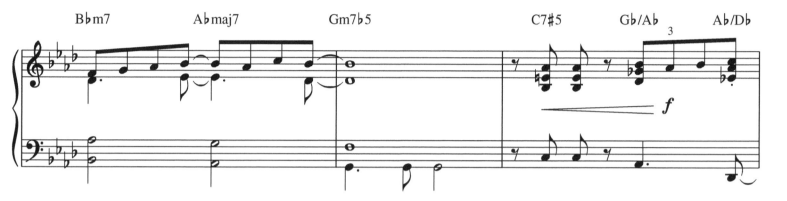

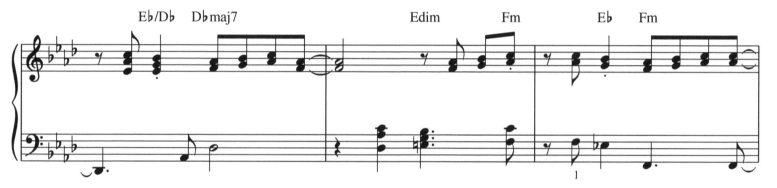

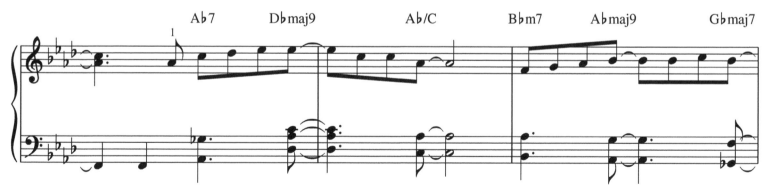

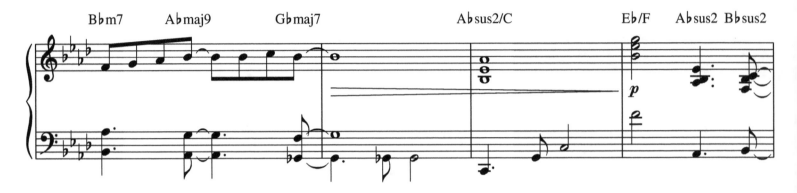

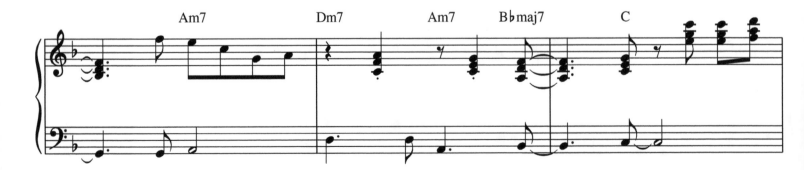

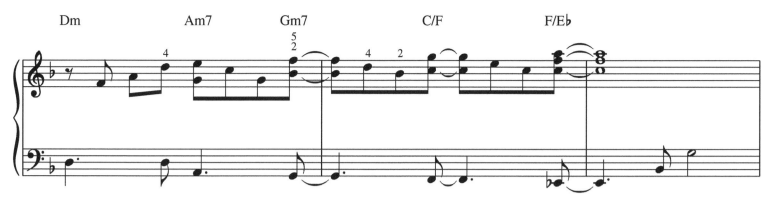

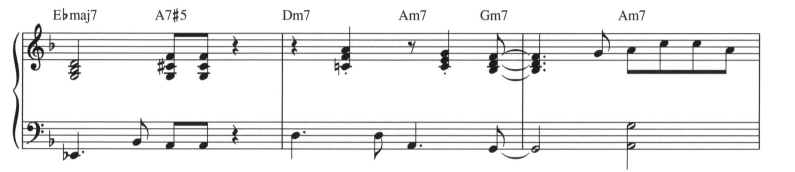

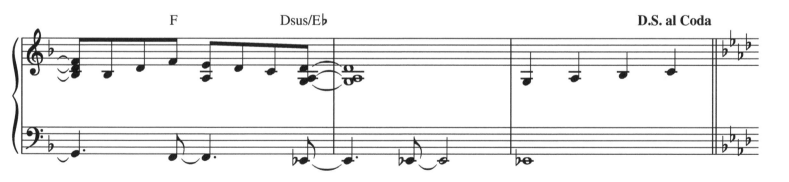

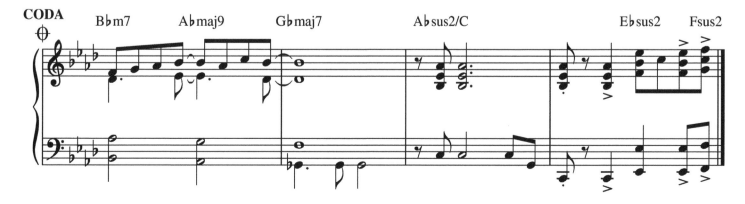

SHE COULD BE MINE

By DON GRUSIN

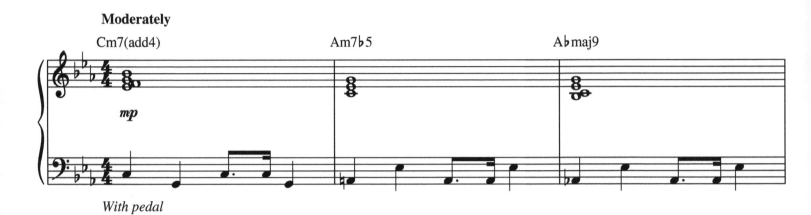

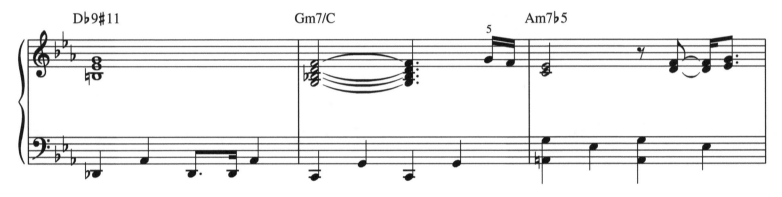

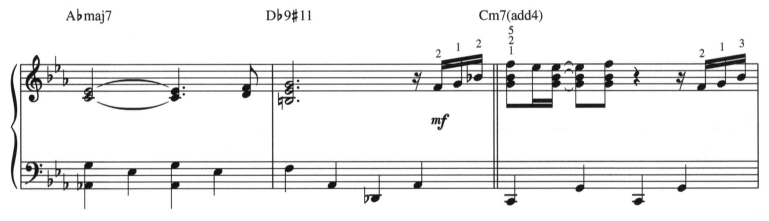

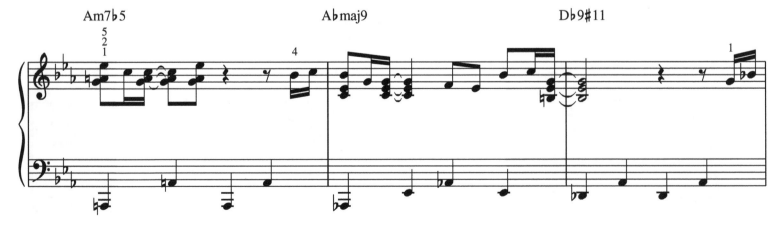

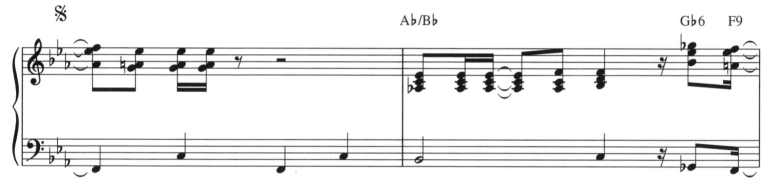

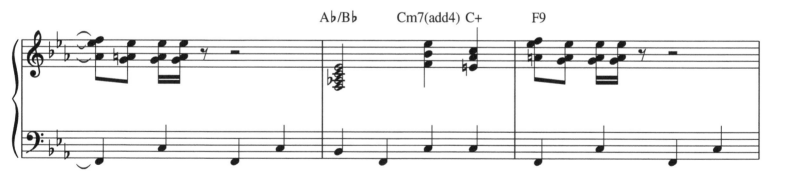

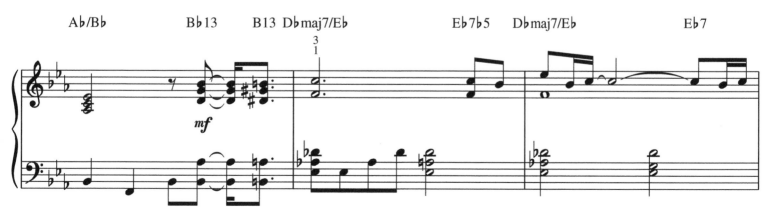

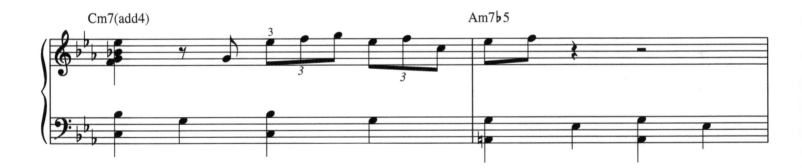

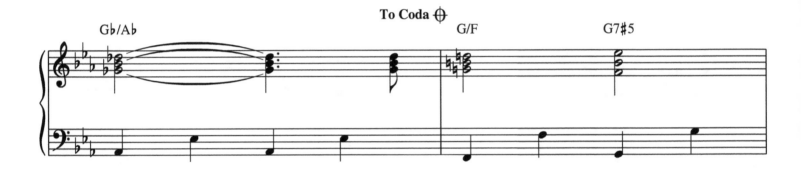

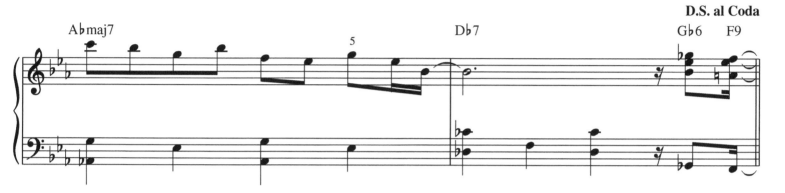

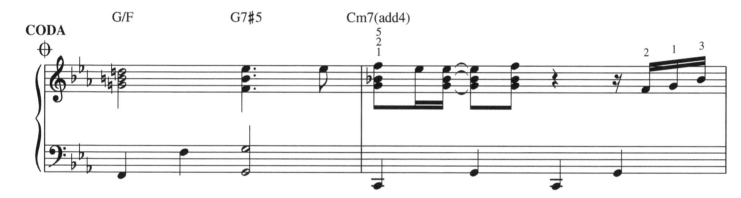

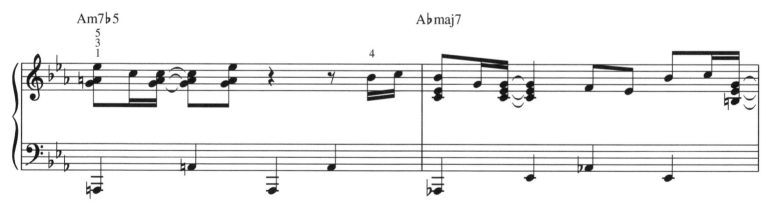

SILHOUETTE

By KENNY G

In a slow 2

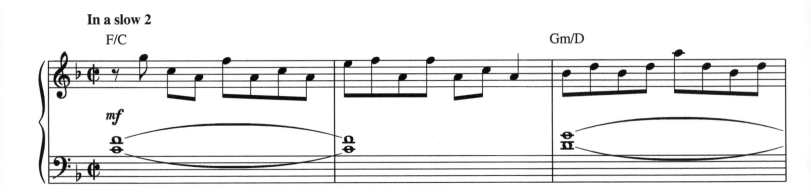

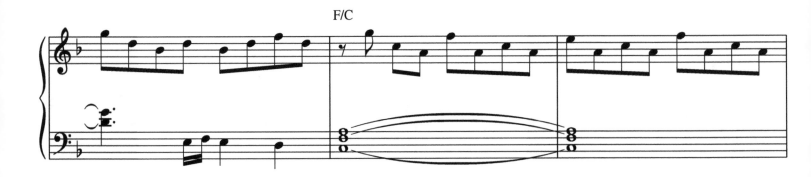

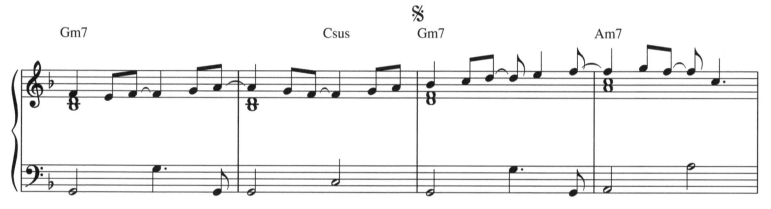

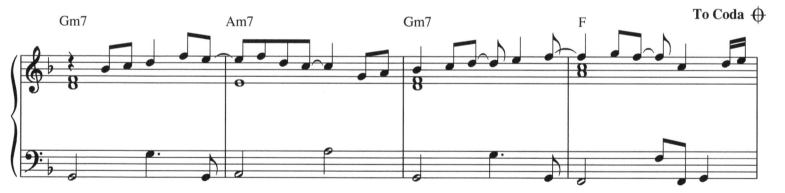

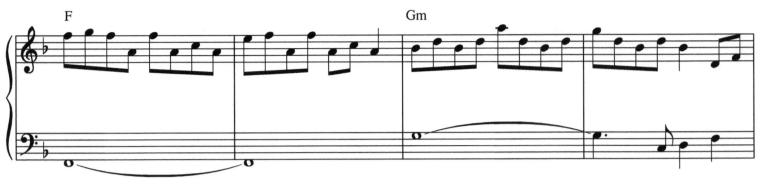

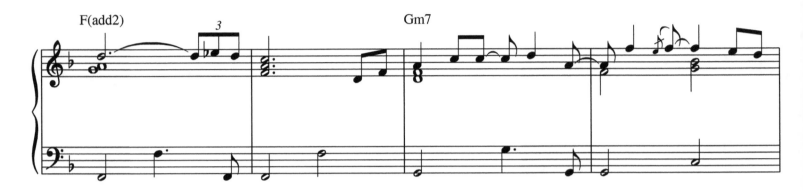

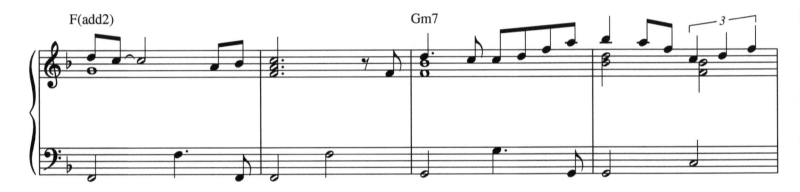

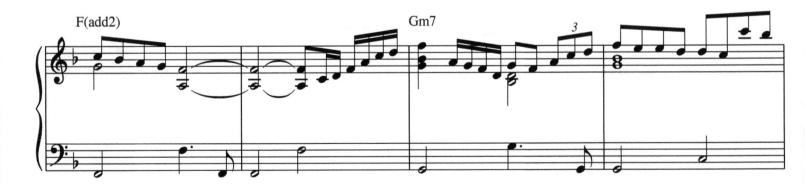

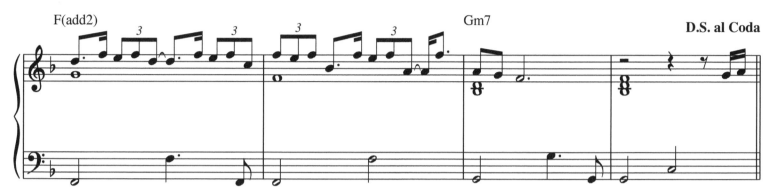

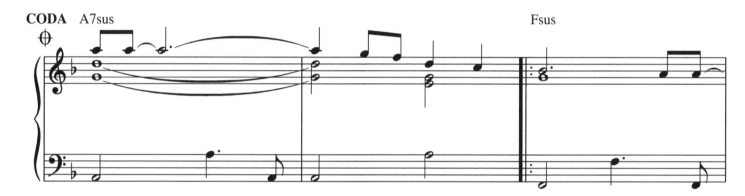

SONGBIRD

By KENNY G

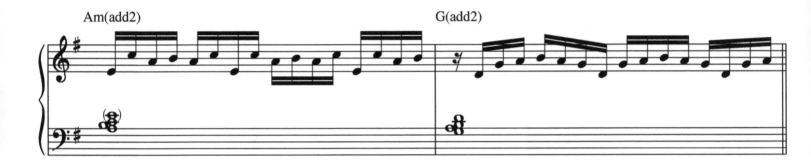

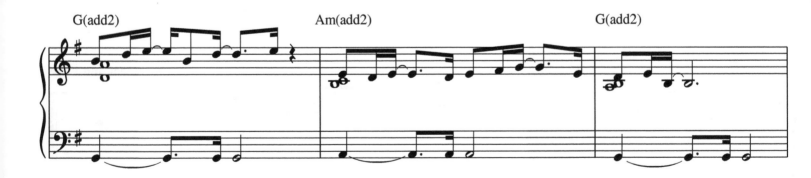

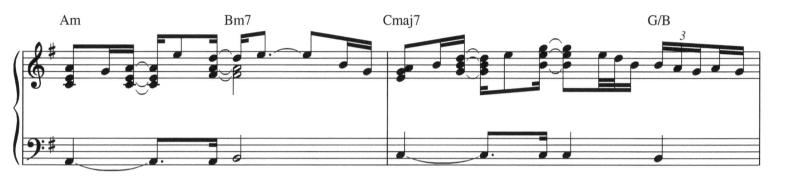

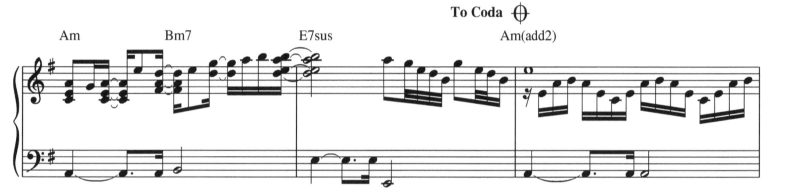

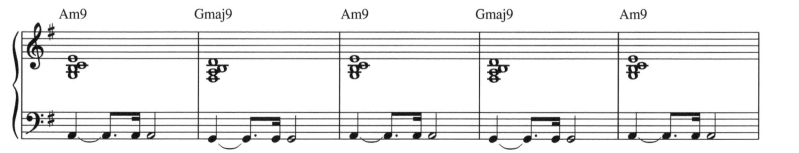

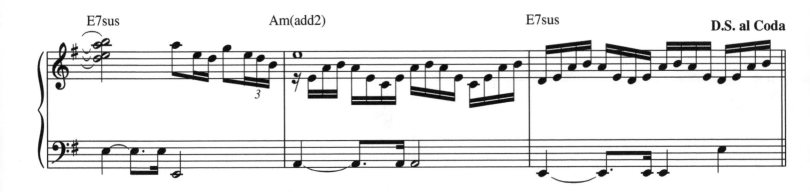

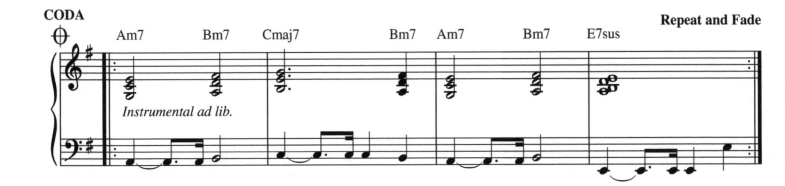

THIS MASQUERADE

Words and Music by
LEON RUSSELL

Moderately

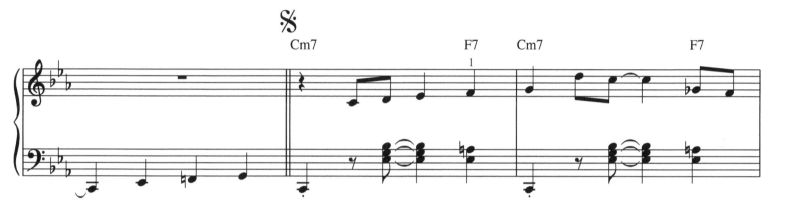

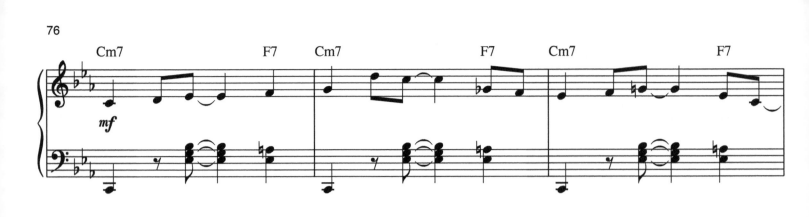

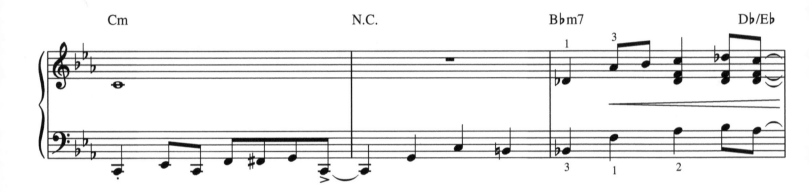

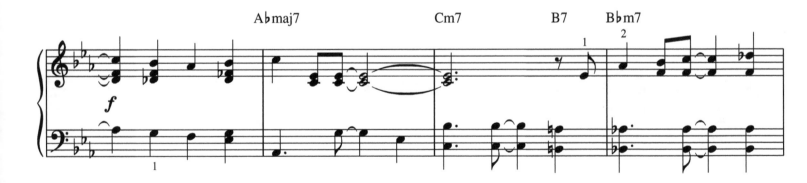

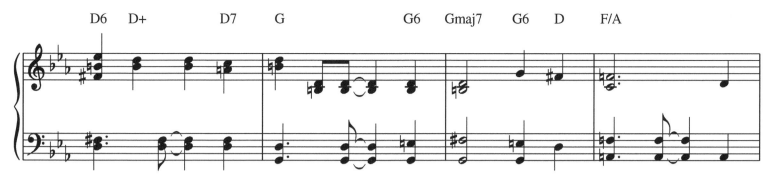

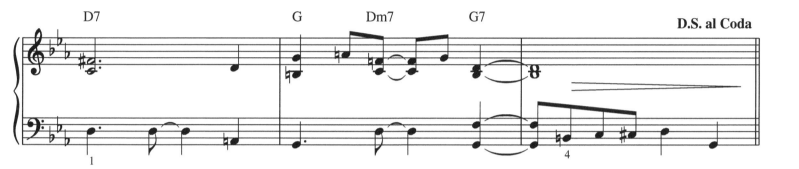

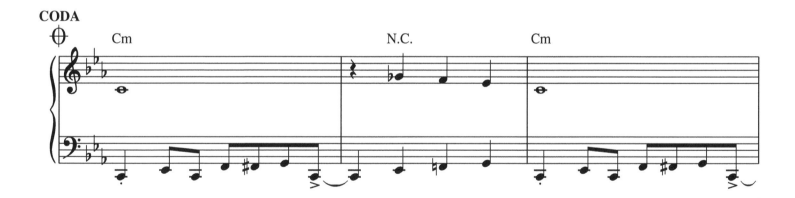

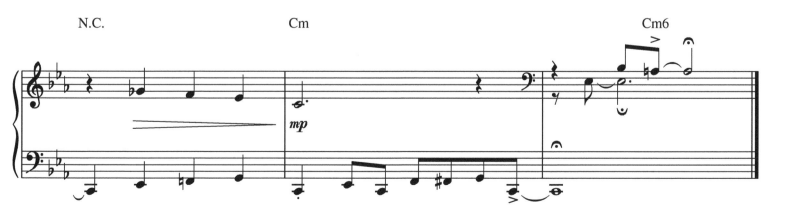

STREET LIFE

Words and Music by WILL JENNINGS
and JOE SAMPLE

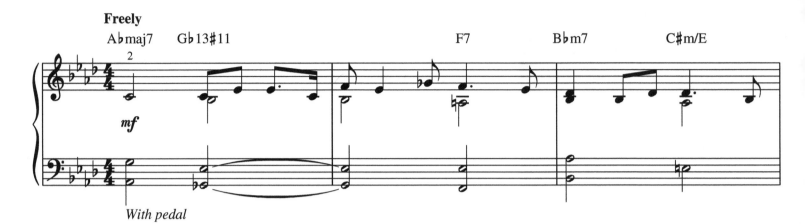

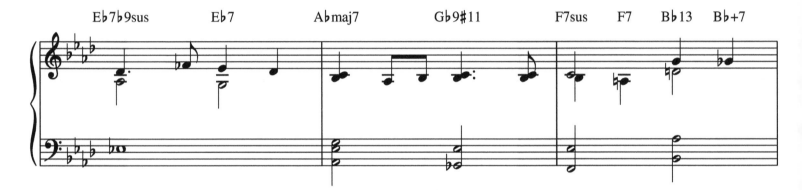

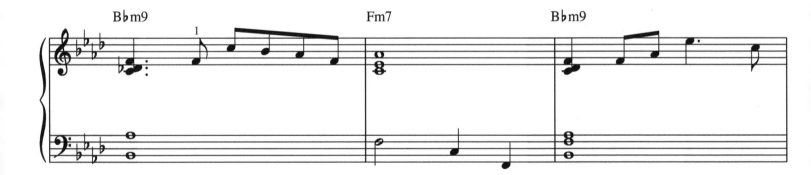

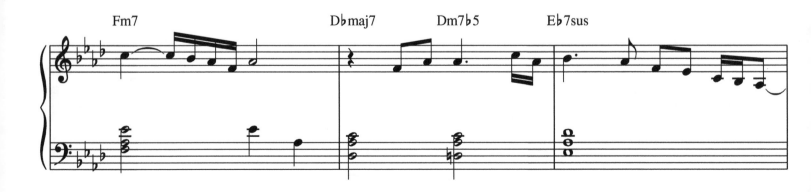

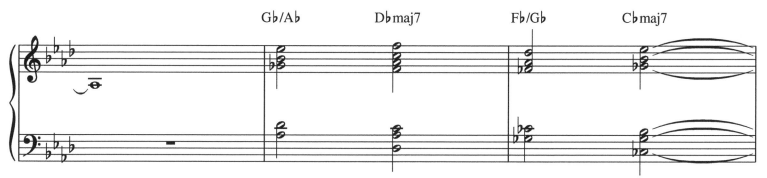

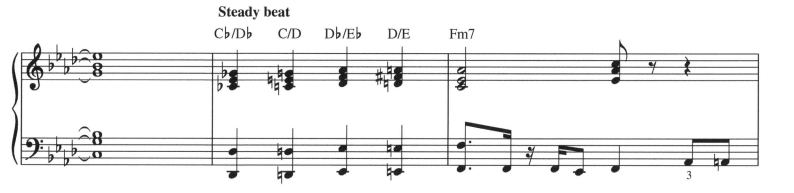

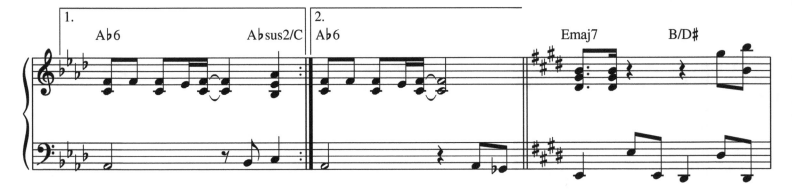

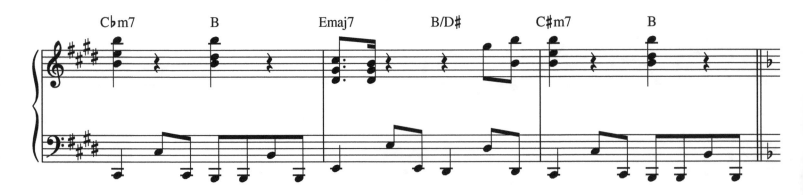

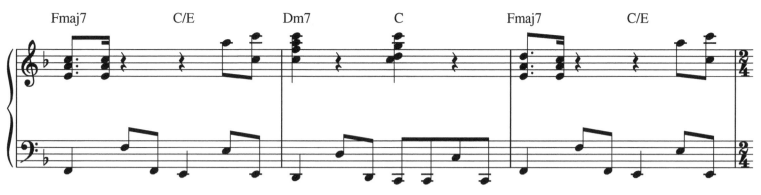

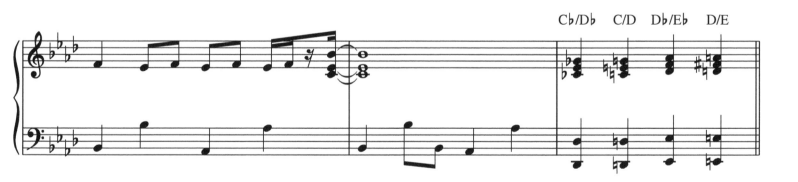

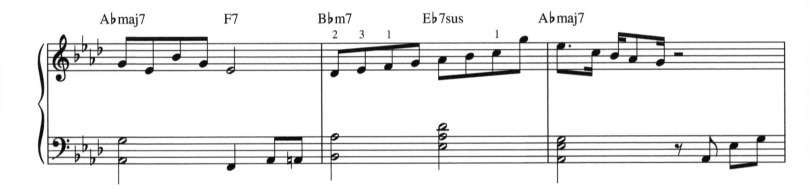

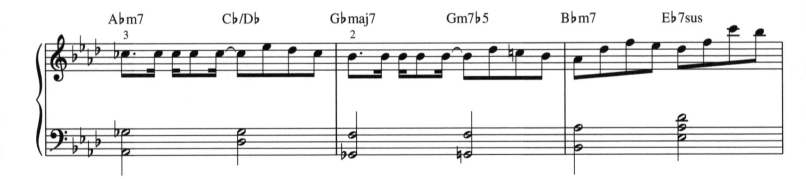

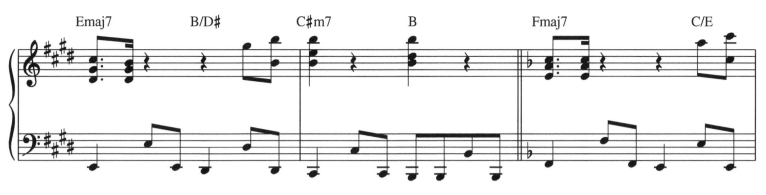

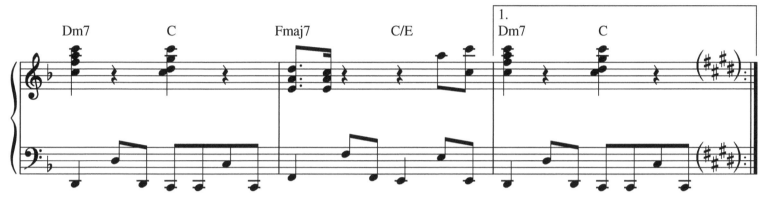

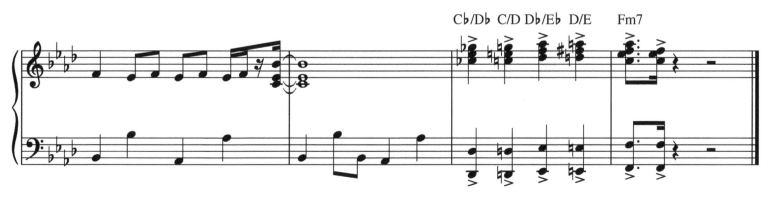

TURN YOUR LOVE AROUND

Words and Music by JAY GRAYDON,
STEVE LUKATHER and BILL CHAMPLIN

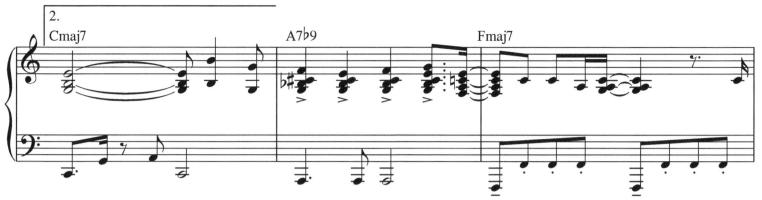

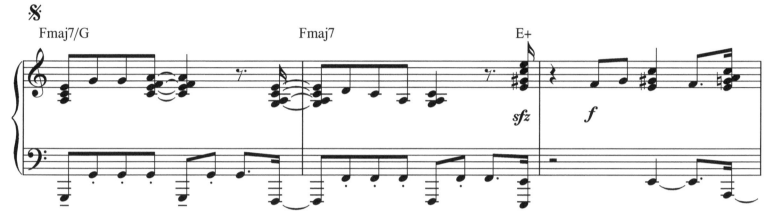

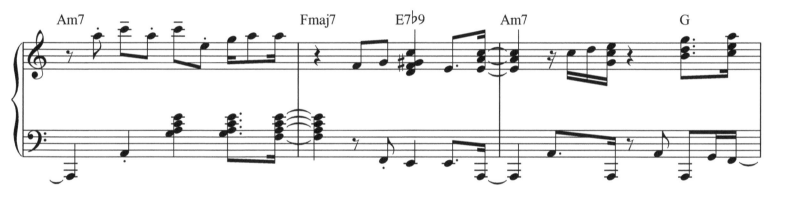

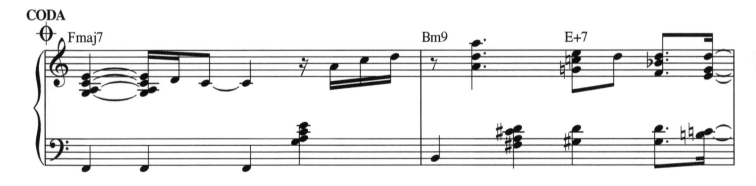

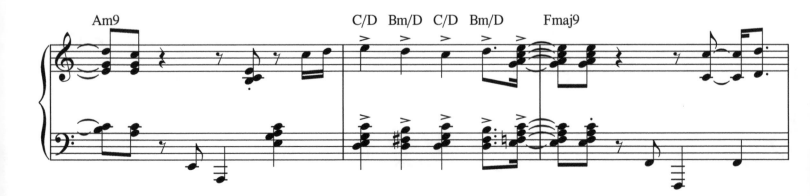

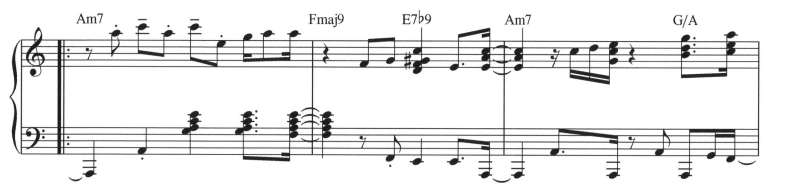

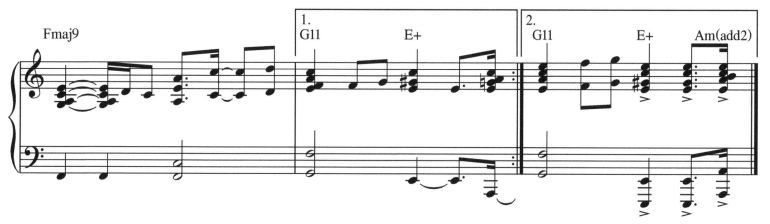

WE'RE IN THIS LOVE TOGETHER

Words and Music by KEITH STEGALL
and ROGER MURRAH

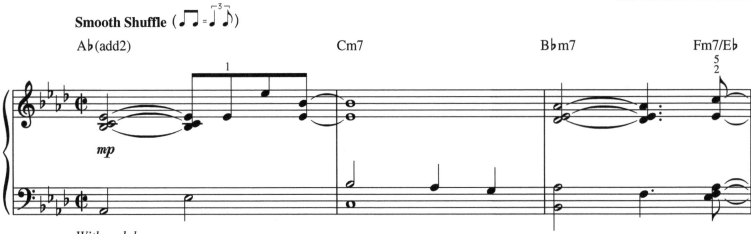

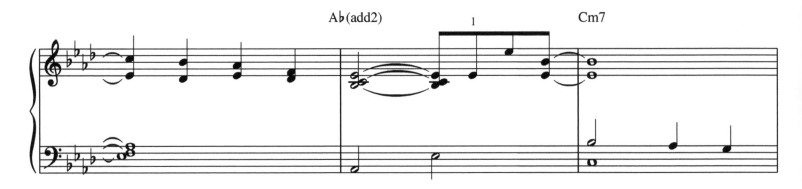

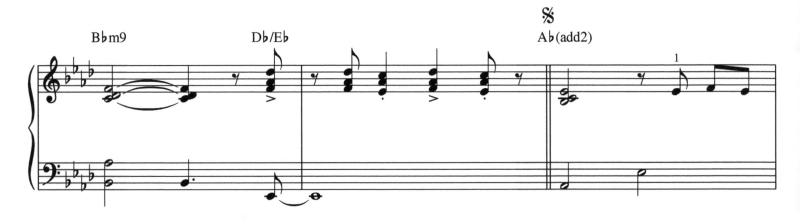

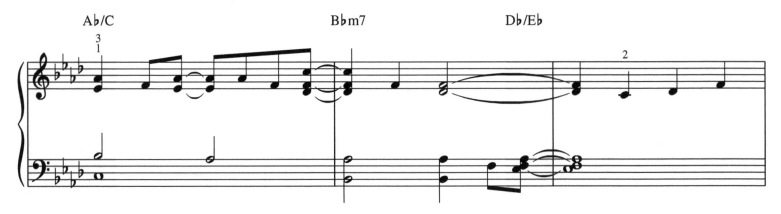

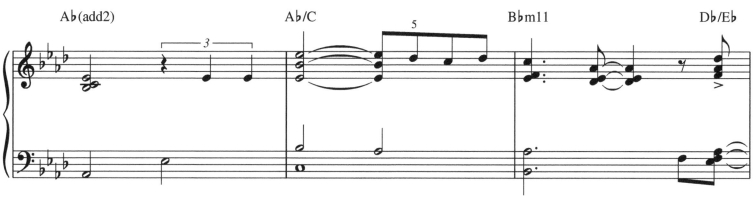

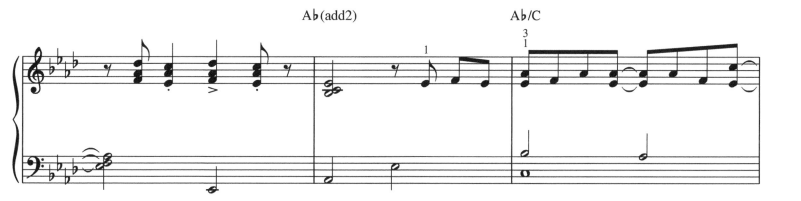

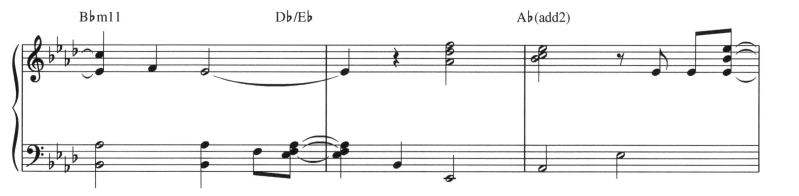

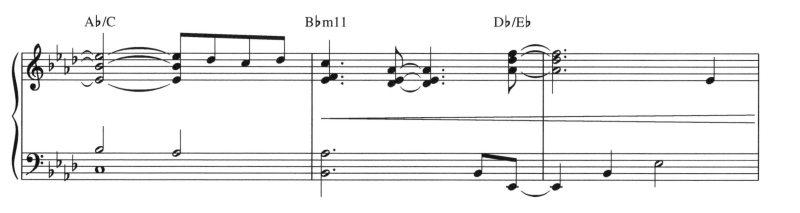

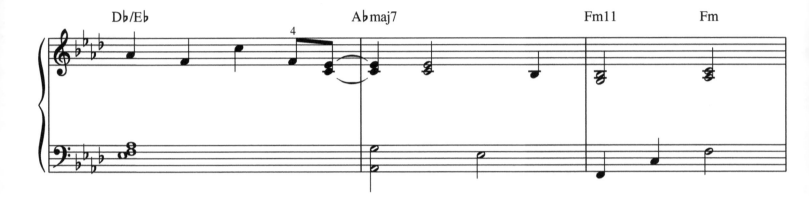

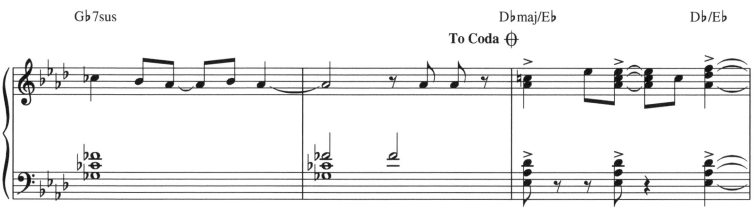

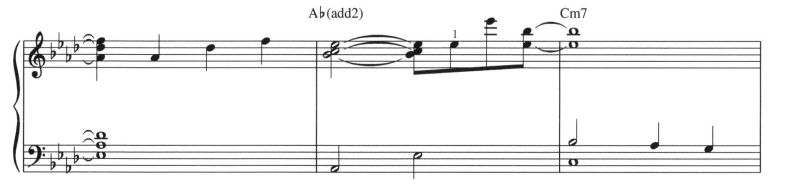

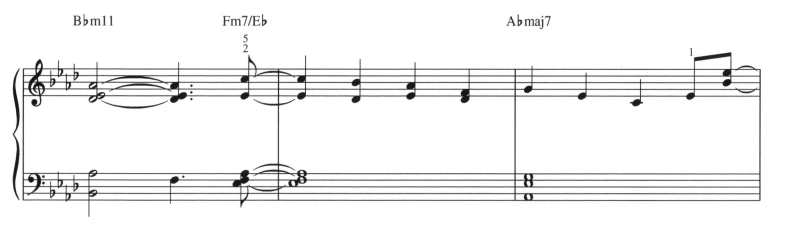

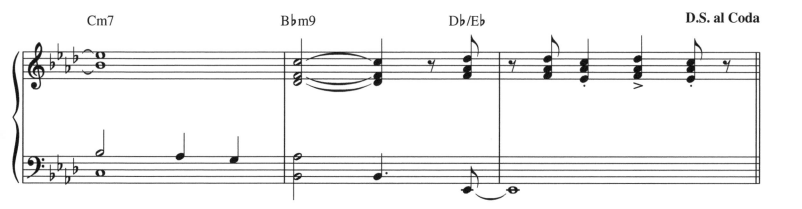

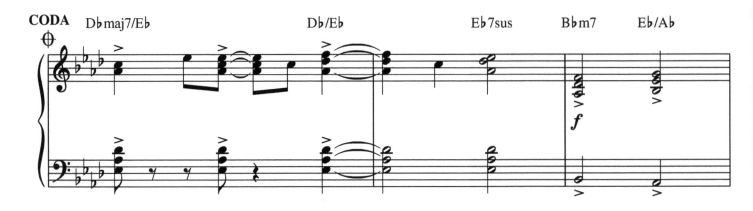

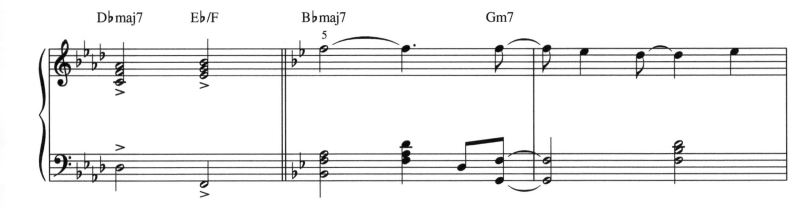

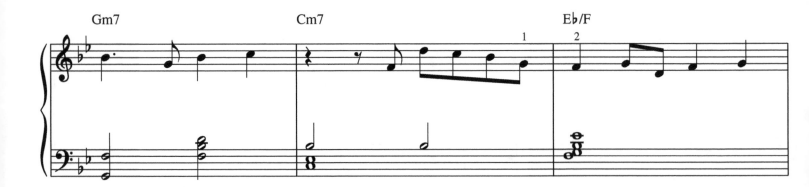

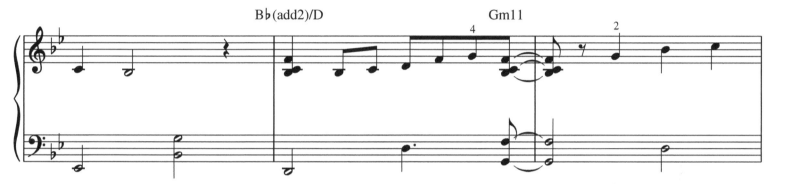

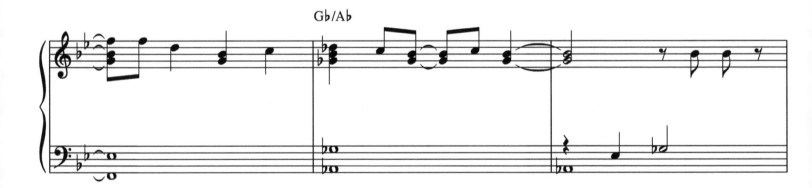

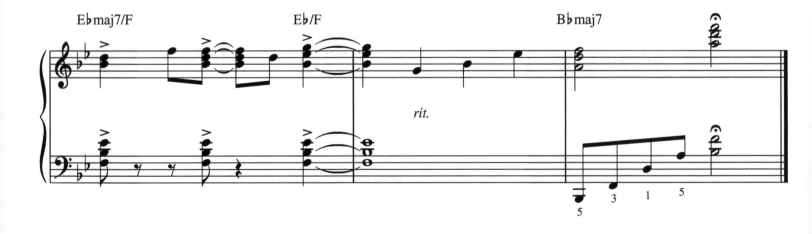

The Best-Selling Jazz Book of All Time Is Now Legal!

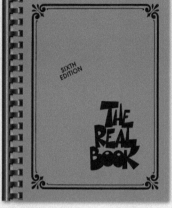

The Real Books are the most popular jazz books of all time. Since the 1970s, musicians have trusted these volumes to get them through every gig, night after night. The problem is that the books were illegally produced and distributed, without any regard to copyright law, or royalties paid to the composers who created these musical masterpieces.

Hal Leonard is very proud to present the first legitimate and legal editions of these books ever produced. You won't even notice the difference, other than all the notorious errors being fixed: the covers and typeface look the same, the song lists are nearly identical, and the price for our edition is even cheaper than the originals!

Every conscientious musician will appreciate that these books are now produced accurately and ethically, benefitting the songwriters that we owe for some of the greatest tunes of all time!

VOLUME 1
00240221 C Edition $45.00
00240224 B♭ Edition $45.00
00240225 E♭ Edition $45.00
00240226 Bass Clef Edition $45.00
00286389 F Edition $39.99
00240292 C Edition 6 x 9 ....$39.99
00240339 B♭ Edition 6 x 9 ....$39.99
00147792 Bass Clef Edition 6 x 9 ....$39.99
00200984 Online Backing Tracks: Selections $45.00
00110604 Book/USB Flash Drive Backing Tracks Pack..............$85.00
00110599 USB Flash Drive Only $50.00

VOLUME 2
00240222 C Edition $45.00
00240227 B♭ Edition $45.00
00240228 E♭ Edition $45.00
00240229 Bass Clef Edition $45.00
00240293 C Edition 6 x 9 ....$39.99
00125900 B♭ Edition 6 x 9 ....$39.99
00125900 The Real Book – Mini Edition $39.99
00204126 Backing Tracks on USB Flash Drive $50.00
00204131 C Edition – USB Flash Drive Pack $85.00

VOLUME 3
00240233 C Edition $45.00
00240284 B♭ Edition $45.00
00240285 E♭ Edition $45.00
00240286 Bass Clef Edition $45.00
00240338 C Edition 6 x 9 ....$39.99

VOLUME 4
00240296 C Edition $45.00
00103348 B♭ Edition $45.00
00103349 E♭ Edition $45.00
00103350 Bass Clef Edition $45.00

VOLUME 5
00240349 C Edition $45.00
00175278 B♭ Edition $45.00
00175279 E♭ Edition $45.00

VOLUME 6
00240534 C Edition $45.00
00223637 E♭ Edition $45.00

Also available:
00154230 The Real Bebop Book $34.99
00240264 The Real Blues Book $39.99
00310910 The Real Bluegrass Book $39.99
00240223 The Real Broadway Book $39.99
00240440 The Trane Book $25.00
00125426 The Real Country Book $45.00
00269721 The Real Miles Davis Book C Edition.........$29.99
00269723 The Real Miles Davis Book B♭ Edition $29.99
00240355 The Real Dixieland Book C Edition $39.99
00294853 The Real Dixieland Book E♭ Edition $39.99
00122335 The Real Dixieland Book B♭ Edition $39.99
00240235 The Duke Ellington Real Book $25.00
00240268 The Real Jazz Solos Book $39.99
00240348 The Real Latin Book C Edition $39.99
00127107 The Real Latin Book B♭ Edition.................$39.99
00120809 The Pat Metheny Real Book C Edition $34.99
00252119 The Pat Metheny Real Book B♭ Edition......$29.99
00240358 The Charlie Parker Real Book C Edition......$25.00
00275997 The Charlie Parker Real Book E♭ Edition $25.00
00118324 The Real Pop Book – Vol. 1 ....$39.99
00240331 The Bud Powell Real Book $25.00
00240437 The Real R&B Book C Edition $45.00
00276590 The Real R&B Book B♭ Edition $45.00
00240313 The Real Rock Book...................................$39.99
00240323 The Real Rock Book – Vol. 2 ....$39.99
00240359 The Real Tab Book $39.99
00240317 The Real Worship Book...............................$35.00

THE REAL CHRISTMAS BOOK
00240306 C Edition $35.00
00240345 B♭ Edition $35.00
00240346 E♭ Edition $35.00
00240347 Bass Clef Edition $35.00
00240431 A-G CD Backing Tracks $24.99
00240432 H-M CD Backing Tracks $24.99
00240433 N-Y CD Backing Tracks $24.99

THE REAL VOCAL BOOK
00240230 Volume 1 High Voice.................................$40.00
00240307 Volume 1 Low Voice $40.00
00240231 Volume 2 High Voice.................................$39.99
00240308 Volume 2 Low Voice $39.99
00240391 Volume 3 High Voice.................................$39.99
00240392 Volume 3 Low Voice $39.99
00118318 Volume 4 High Voice.................................$39.99
00118319 Volume 4 Low Voice $39.99

Complete song lists online at www.halleonard.com

Creative PIANO SOLO

Looking to add some variety to your playing? Enjoy these beautifully distinctive arrangements for piano solo! These popular tunes get new and unique treatments for a fun and fresh presentation. Explore new styles and enjoy these favorites with a bit of a twist! Each collection includes 20 songs for the intermediate to advanced player.

BOHEMIAN RHAPSODY & OTHER EPIC SONGS

Band on the Run • A Day in the Life • Free Bird • November Rain • Piano Man • Roundabout • Stairway to Heaven • Take the Long Way Home • and more.

00196019 Piano Solo.................................$14.99

CHRISTMAS CAROLS

Away in a Manger • Deck the Hall • The First Noel • God Rest Ye Merry, Gentlemen • Hark! the Herald Angels Sing • It Came upon the Midnight Clear • Jingle Bells • Joy to the World • O Holy Night • Silent Night • Up on the Housetop • We Three Kings of Orient Are • What Child Is This? • and more.

00147214 Piano Solo.................................$14.99

CHRISTMAS COLLECTION

Blue Christmas • The Christmas Song (Chestnuts Roasting on an Open Fire) • Frosty the Snow Man • Here Comes Santa Claus (Right down Santa Claus Lane) • Let It Snow! Let It Snow! Let It Snow! • Silver Bells • Sleigh Ride • White Christmas • Winter Wonderland • and more.

00172042 Piano Solo.................................$14.99

CLASSIC ROCK

Another One Bites the Dust • Aqualung • Beast of Burden • Born to Be Wild • Carry on Wayward Son • Layla • Owner of a Lonely Heart • Roxanne • Smoke on the Water • Sweet Emotion • Takin' It to the Streets • 25 or 6 to 4 • Welcome to the Jungle • and more!

00138517 Piano Solo.................................$14.99

Prices, contents, and availability subject to change without notice.

DISNEY FAVORITES

Beauty and the Beast • Can You Feel the Love Tonight • Chim Chim Cher-ee • For the First Time in Forever • How Far I'll Go • Let It Go • Mickey Mouse March • Remember Me (Ernesto de la Cruz) • You'll Be in My Heart • You've Got a Friend in Me • and more.

00283318 Piano Solo.................................$14.99

JAZZ POP SONGS

Don't Know Why • I Just Called to Say I Love You • I Put a Spell on You • Just the Way You Are • Killing Me Softly with His Song • Mack the Knife • Michelle • Smooth Operator • Sunny • Take Five • What a Wonderful World • and more.

00195426 Piano Solo.................................$14.99

JAZZ STANDARDS

All the Things You Are • Beyond the Sea • Georgia on My Mind • In the Wee Small Hours of the Morning • The Lady Is a Tramp • Like Someone in Love • A Nightingale Sang in Berkeley Square • Someone to Watch Over Me • That's All • What'll I Do? • and more.

00283317 Piano Solo.................................$14.99

POP BALLADS

Against All Odds (Take a Look at Me Now) • Bridge over Troubled Water • Fields of Gold • Hello • I Want to Know What Love Is • Imagine • In Your Eyes • Let It Be • She's Got a Way • Total Eclipse of the Heart • You Are So Beautiful • Your Song • and more.

00195425 Piano Solo.................................$14.99

POP HITS

Billie Jean • Fields of Gold • Get Lucky • Happy • Ho Hey • I'm Yours • Just the Way You Are • Let It Go • Poker Face • Radioactive • Roar • Rolling in the Deep • Royals • Smells like Teen Spirit • Viva la Vida • Wonderwall • and more.

00138156 Piano Solo.................................$14.99

HAL•LEONARD®

www.halleonard.com